TWAYNE'S WORLD AUTHORS SERIES

A Survey of the World's Literature

Sylvia E. Bowman, Indiana University

GENERAL EDITOR

FRANCE

Maxwell A. Smith, Guerry Professor of French, Emeritus
The University of Chattanooga
Visiting Professor in Modern Languages
The Florida State University

EDITOR

Jean Anouilh

(TWAS 76)

TWAYNE'S WORLD AUTHORS SERIES (TWAS)

*The purpose of TWAS is to survey the major writers
—novelists, dramatists, historians, poets, philosophers,
and critics—of the nations of the world. Among the
national literatures covered are those of Australia,
Canada, China, Eastern Europe, France, Germany,
Greece, India, Italy, Japan, Latin America, New Zea-
land, Poland, Russia, Scandinavia, Spain, and the
African nations, as well as Hebrew, Yiddish, and
Latin Classical literatures. This survey is complemented by Twayne's United States Authors Series
and English Authors Series.*

*The intent of each volume in these series is to present
a critical-analytical study of the works of the writer;
to include biographical and historical material that
may be necessary for understanding, appreciation,
and critical appraisal of the writer; and to present all
material in clear, concise English—but not to vitiate
the scholarly content of the work by doing so.*

Jean Anouilh

By ALBA DELLA FAZIA

Hunter College
of the
City University of New York

TWAYNE PUBLISHERS
A DIVISION OF G. K. HALL & CO., BOSTON

Library of Congress Catalog Card Number: 68–57245

ISBN 0-8057-2048-0

To the memory of my parents

Preface

A BOUT a decade ago, a New York critic said that, as far as he was concerned, Anouilh and *ennui* were the same thing. Although Americans conveniently (but incorrectly) use this pun to aid them in the pronunciation of Anouilh's rather strange name, the synonymity of the two words has been reasonably dispelled. Jean Anouilh's name has appeared among those suggested for the Nobel Prize for Literature, and today he is acknowledged by some as France's most successful contemporary playwright.

The purpose of this book is to show that, even though similar messages echo and repetitions of idea and form occur in several of Anouilh's works, at no time are the two dozen plays boring or monotonous. Although many of his heroes and heroines are basically stereotypes, they are fascinating in each of their guises. Anouilh's dramas are not unique, but the particular conflicts he creates between illusion and reality, or between good and evil, are unforgettable.

Rather than using the conventional labels of comedy, tragedy, and farce, Anouilh uses the classifications *pièces noires, roses, brillantes, grinçantes,* and *costumées*—"black," "pink," "brilliant," "jarring," and "costumed" plays. These groupings, in the order enumerated, will be retained in the discussion of the plays, for they reflect perfectly Anouilh's kaleidoscopic vision of life.

In his youth, Anouilh tended to see situations as completely black (his realism) or completely pink (his idealism). As an adult, his visions of love, honor, and friendship are "brilliant," but the realities of life and love are "jarring." For the mature man, historical figures may be noble, but history is an eternal farce. Thus Joan of Arc, Thomas à Becket, Henry Plantagenet, Louis XVIII, and Napoleon are "costumed" heroes, true to themselves, but playing their roles in *commedia dell'arte* style.

All the plays that deal with mythological or historical characters will, for purposes of convenience, be discussed together under the heading *pièces costumées*, even though they may have been placed in other categories by the author (*Eurydice*, *Antigone*, and *Médée*, three *pièces noires*; *Pauvre Bitos*, a *pièce grinçante*; *Oreste*, fragments of a 1945 unclassified play). An early unclassified play, *Y avait un prisonnier*, written during the "black" period and similar in many ways to the "black" play *Le Voyageur sans bagage*, will be discussed together with the plays of that category.

Three of Anouilh's later unclassified plays, *L'Hurluberlu* (1959), *La Grotte* (1961), and *L'Orchestre* (1962), will also be placed where they seem most naturally to fit: *L'Hurluberlu* with the *pièces grinçantes*, since the hero, Le Général, is the same character as Le Général in two other "jarring" plays, *Ardèle* and *La Valse des Toréadors*; *La Grotte*, *L'Orchestre* and *Le Boulanger, la Boulangère et le Petit Mitron* with the earlier *pièces noires*, for in them Anouilh seems to have come full circle through the kaleidoscope of tints and tones to return to a completely dark vision of society.

A few insignificant plays such as *Humulus le muet* (1929), *La Petite Molière* (1959), *Madame de . . .* (1959), *Episode de la vie d'un auteur* (1959), and *Le Songe du critique* (1961) will be touched upon only briefly or not at all. Anouilh's other writings— his fables, film scenarios, and a short story—will not be discussed since they contribute in no way to his theatrical reputation.

The sections of this volume are divided thus: a short chronology of the significant dates and facts of Anouilh's life and publications will precede a chapter sketching the life and times of the author solely as they relate to his work. The body of the book will be devoted to the plays themselves. The general picture of Anouilh's dramatic concept and an outline of recurrent themes will be followed by a critical and analytical discussion of the individual plays. The "black," "pink," "brilliant," "jarring," and "costumed" plays will be analyzed in that order, since such a procedure has the advantage referred to above and provides as well an almost chronological development. To aid the reader, a brief résumé of each play under discussion will precede its critical analysis. In those cases where two or more plays are quite similar, the presentation of the less important plays will be limited to brief outlines of plots and characters, and analogies with the predominant play in the group will be drawn subsequently.

Preface

Once the plays have been put into focus, the pages dealing with the underlying characteristics of Anouilh's dramatic technique will have greater significance and the placing of Jean Anouilh's theater in the tradition of the *commedia dell'arte* will be more convincing.

A brief chapter dealing with theatrical and literary influences on Anouilh will give credit where it is due, but hopefully establish the dramatist's originality. The last chapter of the book will attempt to reinforce the thesis of Anouilh's originality by placing his work in a broader perspective, and will serve as a conclusion to this work.

For the sake of consistency, titles of plays are throughout the book left in French. Where English versions have been widely performed, the recognized English title is given in the Chronology. In the descriptions of plot, references of names and details are directly from the original plays, with the exception of the use of English names for mythological, legendary, and historical persons and places.

Translations are my own, unless otherwise noted.

All notes and references will be found at the back of the book.

I wish to express thanks to Professor Sylvia Bowman, Professor Maxwell A. Smith, and Mr. Erik J. Friis; to Professor Bettina Knapp of Hunter College of the City University of New York, whose special knowledge and expertise were of great profit to me; to Dr. Lucille Frackman Becker of Rutgers University and Dr. Maxine Gordon Cutler of Barnard College for their professional advice and criticism; and to Miss Joan Grishman, who helped prepare the manuscript for publication.

My thanks go also to Dr. Franco Amoia and to Dr. and Mrs. Joseph Fiore for having created the conditions both necessary and conducive to the researching and writing of this book.

ALBA DELLA FAZIA

New York, 1968

Contents

Chronology

1910   Born on June 23 in Cérisole, near Bordeaux, France. Jean Anouilh's father was a tailor, his mother a violinist.

1918–   Anouilh's primary and secondary education in Paris at
1927   the Ecole Colbert, and at the Collège Chaptal, where he was a fellow student of Jean-Louis Barrault.

1927–   One and a half years of law studies at the University of
1929   Paris.

1929–   Worked in an advertising agency. Wrote two insignificant
1931   plays: *Humulus le muet* and *Mandarine*. Wrote advertisement scripts and comic gags (at 100 francs per gag) for the films in order to help make ends meet.

1931   Married the actress Monelle Valentin. Wrote *L'Hermine*, his first work to meet with some success; it had its première at the Théâtre de l'Oeuvre in Paris, on April 26, 1932.

1931–   Served as secretary to actor-director Louis Jouvet at the
1932   Comédie des Champs-Elysées in Paris.

1932   Wrote *Le Bal des voleurs* (*Thieves' Carnival*), first performed on September 17, 1938, at the Théâtre des Arts in Paris. Produced at the Cherry Lane Theatre in New York during the 1954–55 season, this play was the first real Anouilh success in the United States.

1934   Wrote *La Sauvage* (*Restless Heart*), first performed on January 10, 1938, at the Théâtre des Mathurins in Paris.

1935   Metro-Goldwyn-Mayer bought the film rights for *Y avait un prisonnier*, which had been produced on March 21, 1935, at the Théâtre des Ambassadeurs in Paris.

1936   Wrote *Le Voyageur sans bagage* (*Traveller Without Luggage*), his first financial stage success. The play had its première on February 16, 1937, at the Théâtre des Mathurins. Rights were bought by Republic Pictures, whose 1945 production entitled *Identity Unknown* was directed by Anouilh himself.

1937   Wrote *Le Rendez-vous de Senlis* (*Dinner with the Family*), first performed on January 30, 1941, at the Théâtre de l'Atelier in Paris.

1939   Wrote *Léocadia* (*Time Remembered*), first performed on November 28, 1940, at the Théâtre de la Michodière in Paris. It was produced in New York during the 1957–58 season and starred Helen Hayes, Richard Burton, and Susan Strasberg.

1940– The Occupation of Paris by the Nazis. Anouilh remained
1944   immersed in his work, declaring that he cared nothing about politics .

1941   Wrote *Eurydice* (*Legend of Lovers*), first performed on December 18, 1941, at the Théâtre de l'Atelier. This play was produced twice in New York, in 1951 and in 1960, but neither the original American production nor the revival had any success.

1942   Wrote *Antigone*, first performed on February 4, 1944, at the Théâtre de l'Atelier. His wife, Monelle Valentin, scored a triumph in the title role. Katherine Cornell played Antigone in the New York production in 1946, but it ran for only sixty-four performances. *Antigone* was included in the repertoire of the American Shakespeare Festival Theatre at Stratford, Connecticut, in 1967.

1947   Wrote *L'Invitation au Château* (*Ring 'Round the Moon*), first performed on November 4, 1947, at the Théâtre de l'Atelier. Christopher Fry's brilliant adaptation of the play met with success in both London and New York.

1948   Wrote *Ardèle* (*Cry of the Peacock*), first performed on November 3, 1948, at the Comédie des Champs-Elysées. The New York production in 1949 closed after two nights, but in 1957 it fared somewhat better.

1950   Wrote two *pièces brillantes: La Répétition* (*The Rehearsal*), first performed on October 25, 1950, at the Théâtre Marigny in Paris, and *Colombe* (*Mademoiselle Colombe*), first performed on February 11, 1951, at the Théâtre de l'Atelier.

1951   Wrote *La Valse des Toréadors* (*The Waltz of the Toreadors*), first performed on January 9, 1952, at the Comédie des Champs-Elysées.

Chronology

1952   Wrote *L'Alouette* (*The Lark*), first performed on October 14, 1952, at the Théâtre Montparnasse-Gaston Baty in Paris. The New York production of the play in 1955 achieved great success with Julie Harris in the role of Joan of Arc.

1953   Anouilh's marriage to Monelle Valentin having ended in divorce, he married on July 30 another actress, Nicole Lançon, whose stage name is Charlotte Chardon.

With Paule de Beaumont, adapted Eugene O'Neill's *Desire Under the Elms* (*Désir sous les ormes*), for production at the Comédie des Champs-Elysées.

1954   Wrote *Cécile, ou l'école des pères,* first performed on October 29, 1954, at the Comédie des Champs-Elysées, starring his daughter, Catherine Anouilh.

With Claude Vincent, adapted Oscar Wilde's *The Importance of Being Earnest* (*Il est important d'être aimé*), for production at the Comédie des Champs-Elysées.

1956   Wrote *Pauvre Bitos* (*Poor Bitos*), first performed on October 11, 1956, at the Théâtre Montparnasse-Gaston Baty. The New York production in 1964 starred Donald Pleasence in the title role.

1957   New York Drama Critics' Circle voted *The Waltz of the Toreadors* (with Sir Ralph Richardson) the best foreign play of the 1956–57 season.

Anouilh and Claude Vincent adapted Shakespeare's *Twelfth Night* (*La Nuit des Rois*) for production at the Toulon Festival.

1958   Wrote *L'Hurluberlu* (*The Fighting Cock*), first performed on February 5, 1959, at the Comédie des Champs-Elysées. The New York production in 1960 with Rex Harrison folded quickly.

1959   Wrote *Becket,* first performed on October 1, 1959, at the Théâtre Montparnasse-Gaston Baty. This play was produced in New York in 1960, with Anthony Quinn in the role of Henry Plantagenet and Laurence Olivier as Thomas à Becket. Film rights were sold to Paramount, whose production starred Richard Burton and Peter O'Toole.

1960   Anouilh staged Molière's *Tartuffe* on November 5 at the Comédie des Champs-Elysées; his own curtain-raiser, *Le Songe du critique,* was written to ward off the critics' censure of him as a stage director.

1962   Wrote *L'Orchestre*, first performed at the Comédie des Champs-Elysées on February 10.

Anouilh achieved marked success as one of France's outstanding *metteurs-en-scène* by his staging of Graham Greene's *The Complacent Lover* and Roger Vitrac's *Victor*, as well as his own plays *La Grotte* (1961) and *La Foire d'empoigne*.

1963   Was reported to have given up playwriting.

1964   Adapted Shakespeare's *Richard III* for production at the Théâtre Montparnasse-Gaston Baty. Anouilh had translated and adapted three other Shakespeare plays, *As You Like It*, *A Winter's Tale*, and *Twelfth Night*, which were published by La Table ronde in 1952. Two of Anouilh's plays were on Broadway during the fall 1964 season: *Traveller Without Luggage* and *Poor Bitos*.

1966   Adapted Kleist's *L'Ordalie ou La Petite Cathrine de Heilbronn* for production at the Théâtre Montparnasse-Gaston Baty.

1967   Revivals of *Pauvre Bitos*, produced by Anouilh and Roland Pietri, and of *L'Alouette*, with Suzanne Flon, during the fall season at the Théâtre de Paris.

1968   Wrote *Le Boulanger, la Boulangère et le Petit Mitron*, first performed at the Comédie des Champs-Elysées on November 14.

CHAPTER 1

The Life and Times of Jean Anouilh

NOW in his late fifties and with over two dozen produced plays to his credit, Jean Anouilh enjoys a popularity which, since World War II, has spread far beyond the Parisian theatrical district and into many foreign countries. His plays, which range from the lightest comedy to the deepest tragedy, are vivid and haunting, demonstrating Anouilh's skill in creating unforgettable characters who are at the same time both individualized and symbolic.

Despite his fame, little is known about Anouilh's private life. He lives today in elegant seclusiveness, at times in a sumptuous Left Bank apartment, at times in his various dwellings in Neuilly and other Parisian suburbs. The few details of Anouilh's life that are available, however, are important in explaining some of the obsessive themes that are an outgrowth of his early environment.

I *Early Life*

Anouilh was born on June 23, 1910, in a small town near Bordeaux in the southwest of France. His earliest years coincided with the pre-World War I era which has been labeled "the last period of bourgeois security in France." [1] World War I was destined to upset many of the deep-seated and undisputed moral traditions and spiritual beliefs of the social class that Anouilh came to despise; by the end of the war, the so-called "civilized" bourgeoisie was detested and attacked on all sides by a disenchanted postwar generation. The typical bourgeois family became a butt of ridicule, and Anouilh was to use bourgeois family scenes to express his contempt and scorn for the vulgar and hypocritical middle class.

The plots of Anouilh's plays stem from psycho-sociological factors; the author belonged to the generation of youth raised during World War I, and having known poverty in his childhood, he was always to remember its effects. The former circumstance probably influenced the formation of the Anouilh hero; the latter was the most likely source of inspiration for his bitter and dismal *pièces noires.*

French society during the years 1914–1918 was composed mainly of women and priests. Children were exposed to a twofold experience which stressed on the one hand affection and sensitivity, on the other humility and inaction. Besides feeling the absence of comradeship provided by ideal father-son relationships, the World War I generation of children was also deprived of close-at-hand "father images"—energetic, strong-willed men whose example could be followed. This may account for the fact that Anouilh's heroes and heroines are physically weak and womanish.

Molded in softness, both Anouilh's male and female characters are aware of their detestable yet unalterable effeminate delicacy. Le Général, a misnamed character in several of Anouilh's plays, would like to be strong and virile, to be able to stand up to society's bullies; Joan of Arc in *L'Alouette* would be only too content to have been born a man so that she might mount her horse and lead Frenchmen into battle with more decorum; Medea laments: "O sun . . . why did you make me a girl? Why these breasts, this weakness? . . . Wouldn't a male Medea have been handsome? Wouldn't he have been strong? A body hard as stone . . . firm, intact, unbroken. . . . Woman! Woman! Bitch! Flesh made of a little clay and the rib of a man! A scrap of man!" [2]

The physical weakness of Anouilh's heroes is in sharp contrast to their strength of character, and this polarity produces within them a conflict which isolates them and renders them what society calls "maladjusted" individuals. They are doubly handicapped: by physical weakness, and by shame at their poverty—both of which condemn them to solitude. In this respect, they are an incarnation or reflexion of the author's own youth.

Anouilh was an introspective child with romantic tendencies, and this was accentuated by the anachronism of childhood days spent in an adult environment. When he was eight years old, one of his relatives, who was the director of the Casino at Arcachon (a summer resort in the southwest of France), hired Anouilh's mother, a violinist, to play in the orchestra. Every night during the three-month engagement, young Anouilh sat unobtrusively in the Casino listening to the operettas until his bedtime. In this milieu he acquired a true sense of the stage, but he also must have been aware that his mother earned little more than a free round of drinks for her work in the Casino.

The deep impression the Casino orchestra made on Anouilh is revealed by the many poor musicians in his plays: the heroine of *La Sauvage* is a café violinist; the entire cast of *L'Orchestre* are cheap café musicians; Orpheus' father (*Eurydice*) and Madame de Montalembreuse (*Le Rendez-vous de Senlis*) are both aging musicians who pride themselves on having won second prize in the Arcachon Conservatory in their younger days—an award that was of no help in escaping their sordid milieu.

If Anouilh's family environment offered no opportunity to form close friendships with boys of his own age, he himself seemed to show no inclination to make friends at school, either in Bordeaux or later in Paris. The actor and director Jean-Louis Barrault has described Anouilh as being solitary, silent, and distant during their days together in secondary school.[3]

Anouilh must have felt acutely this lack of companionship and friendship, however, for his most famous and perhaps his best play is a drama of friendship (between Becket and King Henry II); there are also many plays in which Anouilh idealizes the intimate relationship between two young boys who would risk their lives for each other, share their loves, and solemnly swear allegiance to each other by mixing their blood, blood drawn from self-inflicted, rusty penknife gashes. Such a friendship existed between the Count and Héro in *La Répétition* when they were school children, but the fact that it was lost soon after they donned long trousers implies that ideal friendship cannot long endure in adult society.

II *The Young Dramatist*

In his adolescence, Anouilh began writing verse plays in the style of Edmond Rostand, the romantic playwright of the turn of the nineteenth century, famous for such fanciful, colorful dramas as *L'Aiglon* and *Cyrano de Bergerac*. At the age of sixteen, Anouilh wrote his first full-length, still unpublished play.

Although he was influenced by Romanticism, other trends more in vogue during Anouilh's early attempts at playwriting were to mark his subsequent works. Conventionalized, realistic "slice of life" plays, as conceived by Antoine and other members of the

Théâtre Libre (founded in 1887), and the commercial theater known as the Théâtre du Boulevard, dedicated to the entertainment of popular audiences, were to wield their influence on Anouilh; his early endeavors, the *pièces noires*, were a combination of melodrama and naturalism.

During Anouilh's early adulthood, poverty seemed still to prevent him from fully developing his personality and displaying his talents. His work for an advertising agency rewarded him sparingly financially, but richly in instruction in the art of precision and ingenuity. Writing advertising slogans, he once commented, is wonderful preparation for writing theatrical cues.[4] Anouilh's replacement of Georges Neveux as secretary to the actor-director Louis Jouvet brought the ex-law-student, ex-advertisement-and-film-comic-gag-writer into the bosom of the theatrical world, yet the experience hindered his efforts to devote himself exclusively to a dramatic career.

At the age of twenty-one, Anouilh married the actress Monelle Valentin. A "make do" policy, but with a fanciful touch, governed his early married life: the stage sets for Jean Giraudoux's *Siegfried*, which was being produced by Jouvet, were loaned to the newlyweds to furnish their apartment. When their daughter was born, a stage-set dresser drawer served as her crib. *Siegfried* was everywhere, Anouilh reminisces: "I knew the play by heart, and Jouvet's intonations resounded so clearly in my ears that I could imitate them." [5] *Siegfried* furnished not only the Anouilh apartment but also, as will be noted below, the inspiration for the writer's third *pièce noire, Le Voyageur sans bagage.*

The oppressive weight of poverty was on Anouilh's shoulders, particularly with a wife and a child to support, until Hollywood's purchase of the film rights for *Le Voyageur sans bagage* brought him sufficient funds for a home and a car. Anouilh's taste of financial success was bittersweet, however, for he considered himself first and foremost a dramatist and was unhappy about lending his characters to the cinema, even though the medium became an important source of income for him.[6] He expresses his scorn of the movies through two of his characters in *Le Rendez-vous de Senlis:* the actor Philémon and the actress Madame de Montalembreuse, who refuse to play their assigned roles unless they receive assurances that the production is for the stage. Looking down their noses at the movies, they relegate to "transatlantic talent"

(Hollywood) the medium that eliminates challenges and denies the true essence of theater—the contact and vibrations between actors and audience.

By this time, Anouilh had obviously undergone a third dramatic influence—that of the "Théâtre de l'Art," fathered by Jacques Copeau in 1913 on the stage of the Vieux Colombier Theater and led by such men as Louis Jouvet, Charles Dullin, Georges Pitoëff, and subsequently Gaston Baty. These *metteurs-en-scène* were seeking a "new truth" and a "pure theater." Their vehicle was the experimental theater, which favored simple stage sets and a highly synthesized production. They tried to bring back into modern drama the poetry and imagination of the classical theater that had been stifled by realism, popular melodrama, and the vaudeville artifices of "*boulevardisme.*"

Dramatists turned to religion, legend, myth, and fantasy in their search for poetry. Audiences were to be invited to dream between the lines in a most personal way, while the *metteur-en-scène* would use all of the technical devices at his command to achieve a unified interpretation. The net result would be an expansion of dramatic form and content. Paul Claudel, André Obey, Jean Cocteau, and Jean Giraudoux were some of the poetic dramatists who helped to fill the new expanded frontiers of pure theater. It was Jouvet who had seized upon the stylized, fanciful, and highly poetic plays of Jean Giraudoux, the dramatist whose romantic tendencies Anouilh admired.

The influence of Giraudoux's magical and musical poetic drama, coupled with Anouilh's release from poverty, revealed a new facet of the playwright's personality. He shifted from a pessimistic ("black") to a more optimistic ("rosy") frame of reference during the years 1937–1939, when two *pièces roses, Le Rendez-vous de Senlis,* and *Léocadia,* were written, and when *Le Bal des voleurs,* the first *pièce rose,* was produced (1938). Giraudoux's influence is manifest in the overall atmosphere of fancy and in the poetic dialogue of these escapist comedies in a theatrical vein.

III *Occupation of Paris and Liberation*

Despite this spurt of optimism, the outbreak of World War II and the subsequent Nazi occupation of Paris (1940–1944) returned Anouilh to his isolation of earlier years. Although he refrained from taking an active part in the occupied capital's conflict, it haunted him. The mood of dark despair that permeated the city was reflected in the *nouvelles pièces noires: Eurydice* (1941), *Antigone* (1942), *Roméo et Jeannette* (1945), and *Médée* (1946). The 1942 play, *Antigone,* was a clear indication that Anouilh felt involved politically: the heroine represents the choice between resistance and collaboration—a painful choice which was to be dramatized once again in *Becket* (1958).

When *Antigone* was first presented in Paris at the Théâtre de l'Atelier on February 4, 1944, a polemic arose concerning the interpretation of the play and the significance of the two main characters. For many, Antigone symbolized the anti-Nazi Resistance movement; she was a glorious heroine for having said "no" to Creon, the symbol of an external order unjustly imposed. Others labeled the play pro-Nazi; they saw in Creon, who pleads movingly for a compromise that will allow him to continue steering the ship of state, an eloquent champion of the Vichy government's thesis of expediency. For them, Creon was an intelligent organizer, more fascinating than Antigone because whereas she refuses to grow up and learn that not everything in life is rosy, he courageously accepts life in its ugliness. Although Anouilh never publicly took sides in the polemic, his sympathy for Antigone can be inferred from other plays, notably *Becket,* in which the heroes and heroines clearly take the extremely conservative position of non-compromise.

In any case, the partisans of Antigone triumphed over those of Creon, and the play continued to fire audiences of patriotic Parisians until the Liberation. The popularity of the play during this period exceeded that of any other because of the politically tense atmosphere and the identification between audience and heroine. Postwar productions of *Antigone* lost their impact, and the London and New York productions of the drama met with only moderate success.

Pauvre Bitos, although written in 1956, deals with the same period and theme. The play takes place in the aftermath of the Liberation, with flashbacks to the French Revolution. It describes a dinner at which a local liquidator of collaborators is given some brutal hints that his methods are making him unpopular. The parallel between the attitudes of some French Revolutionary leaders and provincial French politics of 1945 created a furor when

Pauvre Bitos opened in Paris. The author decided to withhold foreign distribution rights for eight years, but he finally submitted to
the idea that French "dirty laundry" could be washed on non-
Gallic stages, and in 1964 *Poor Bitos* was produced with some
success in London and New York.

IV   *The Brilliant Recluse*

Although the post-Liberation era brought to light Anouilh's
"brilliant" plays (*L'Invitation au Château*, 1947; *La Répétition*,
1950; *Colombe*, 1951; *Cécile*, 1954), the writer's social life, well
removed from Parisian theatrical society, was far from brilliant. A
key to the playwright's social behavior can be found in a curtain-
raiser written and staged in 1949, *Episode de la vie d'un auteur*.
This one-act play has not much dramatic importance, but it
shows vividly how an author and his work suffer by constant
interruption. Anouilh expresses his demands for a private life and
for the possibility of nourishing literary creations in solitude. He
also uses this play to voice his criticisms of the inanity and decadence of Parisian society life—most evident in *L'Hurluberlu*
(1959), the vehicle through which he advocates man's flight from
social life to confinement within the walls of his work and his
family life. Julien, his spokesman in *Colombe*, states: "No, I am
not sociable. But I have made a world for myself, where everything is harder and purer." [7]

Some of the most repelling things that Anouilh saw in Parisian
mores were sexual aberrations, promiscuity and homosexuality,
which constitute the religion of the modern world. The flippant
young blade in *L'Hurluberlu*, David Edward Mendigalès, is a
representative of this new faith. The conservative and shy Anouilh
uses David Edward to show his distaste for Parisian pleasures:
night clubs serviced by nobility, meetings with abstract painters,
communists, dancers, Dominican opium eaters, millionaires, ho-
mosexuals, and the French version of Elsa Maxwell—all of them
of course, very progressive, very evolved, very "crypto."

A society such as this repels Anouilh and he uses it to illustrate
his reasons for taking refuge in the limited circle of his family.
Even friends disenchant him. The protagonist of *L'Hurluberlu*, Le
Général, who has been abandoned by his supporters and friends
in his attempts to restore virtue to France, turns to his wife with

the words: "There will be nothing left to us but ourselves and our children. That's a lot. It's the world. . . . The world is big with two people in it."[8]

Anouilh's reclusion is a flight from the world and also a search for what he has dramatized in so many of his plays: the understanding of one's inner self. The Archbishop's description of Becket also fits Anouilh: "His is a strange, unseizable soul. I have often observed him, in the midst of pleasures and noise. He is as though absent. He is looking for himself."[9] He refuses to don the masks that society imposes on us, and is avoiding the dichotomy, described by one of his heroines, between the public and private personality: "You are a loyal man, but you have two or three personalities and you get confused sometimes."[10]

Despairing of ever reconciling human aspirations and the possibility of their realization, Anouilh lives a life that emphasizes man's inner isolation. False personality and the relationships that society forces upon us cannot conceal man's basic isolation. To our social contacts, others bring *their* false personality. Anouilh feels free to reject other people's values and to follow his own inner convictions—a choice which has resulted in a code of conventions that has marked him as antisocial, amoral, and negativistic.

Just as, in his passivity, Anouilh cherishes no illusions that an ideal social order will ever descend upon this earth, he is in the same way pessimistic about the political situation. Taking refuge in extreme conservatism, he rejects all hopes for the future; his only hopes seem to lie in individuals who are true to themselves. He expresses these sentiments in *L'Invitation au Château:* "We are too careless. I can understand it in politics. You have to let yourself be governed just as you have to have your hair cut—by others, willy-nilly. Attaching too much importance to the money people take from you, or to the gestures required of you, in the streets, by the police, is the most futile, the most thoughtless attitude possible."[11] Although Anouilh is passive with respect to society's futile demands, he is not so with respect to his own destiny: "But to allow destiny to lead you . . . that's serious . . . it's unpardonable."[12]

In his most recent plays, Anouilh sees France crawling with worms. He would like to plot a takeover by a strict oligarchy that would stop the decay of his country. He would trust the scrupulousness only of what he calls an "active minority" of extreme conservatives who would set a plague on all political houses and lead France back to her pristine grandeur—to the pre-progressive, pre-scientific, pre-egalitarian days. Anouilh would teach this minority of Frenchmen two concepts: honor and moral rigor. By dying for something incomprehensible to the masses, a small "race" of men —the "active minority"—has earned the respect of the majority throughout the ages.

Having been bitterly disillusioned in his youthful yearnings for true democracy, Anouilh feels that it is in the world of the past that hope now lies (but he discovers this only *a posteriori*), with its clear separation of rich and poor, with each class (or "race," as he refers to them) adhering to its own tradition and ideals. A French critic has written: "Anouilh's political skepticism is complete—anarchist, destroyer, repudiator, passionate individualist, he rejects the concept of a human collectivity capable of governing itself. He does not believe in the virtue of the people who know only how to be led by the nose. He glorifies the individual act." [13]

This is why, in *Pauvre Bitos*, Anouilh condemns Robespierre's fixed idea that the people, the mediocre masses, are right and that he must act in their name. To protest against the arbitrary choice of victims of the Revolution, Robespierre answers that the arbitrariness of kings is a crime, but the arbitrariness of the people or their representatives is sacred—the exact opposite of Anouilh's belief. The General in *L'Hurluberlu* represents the ideal of the past and the glorification of the individual act, as does, more humbly but just as nobly, the kitchen aide in a later play, *La Grotte*. The latter's painful efforts to remove every eye from the potatoes whose peelings must be as thin as cigarette paper, and his rigid stand for perfection against those who argue that it does not much matter once the potatoes are mashed, are analogous to the General's efforts to restore France to her former virtue.

Harold Clurman, too, has described Anouilh as "an anarchist of the Right, which is hardly any kind of politics, . . . inclined to romanticize a halcyon past and in a crisis do his best to avoid any kind of partisanship." [14] Anouilh, however, is shrewd and realistic enough to know that any fellow conspirers he might be lucky enough to find would ultimately abandon him; that any absurd little oligarchic "underground" plot would fail; that the romantic idealist will have to stand alone in denouncing the worm-riddled world to the walls of his ancient castle. Quixotism and inflexibility have no place in the modern world, Anouilh realizes, and political truths are relative. It is a matter of chance whether those who perform their duties will be honored or dishonored. The individualist's position is both tragic and ludicrous, yet the vision of supreme fidelity to one's cause is not easily effaced.

V *The Playwright's Other Face*

Although Anouilh was driven to solitude during the war and after the liberation, he was nevertheless concerned enough about his art to appear faithfully at rehearsals of his plays in the Paris theaters, much like Count Tigre in the "brilliant" *La Répétition,* the piece in which the characters are rehearsing a Marivaux play under the relentless eye of the ubiquitous Count. The author's presence at these rehearsals was not always relished, as witnessed by the resignation of four of the Théâtre de l'Atelier's cast during rehearsals of *Colombe,* and Jean-Louis Barrault's and Madeleine Renaud's suffering throughout Anouilh's cruel and nerve-wracking expressions of boredom with the Barrault version of *La Répétition.* It is because the sequestered, eremitic Anouilh lives vicariously through his characters and because he himself is such an extraordinary actor[15] that he is so demanding of those who perform in his plays; more recently, however, his criticisms have mellowed and Parisian actors find him more congenial, thus fostering a harmonious relationship between the players and Anouilh in his new role, that of stage director.

From early 1948 Anouilh worked in close collaboration with Roland Pietri, the director of the Comédie des Champs-Elysées, where the playwright's first *pièce grinçante, Ardèle,* was produced on November 4. Subsequently, a *pièce rose* (*Cécile, ou l'Ecole des pères*) and the other three *pièces grinçantes* (*La Valse des Toréadors,* 1952; *Ornifle,* 1955; *Pauvre Bitos,* 1956) were also staged by Pietri. In 1959 the production of *Becket, ou l'Honneur de Dieu* at the Théâtre Montparnasse-Gaston Baty saw Pietri and Anouilh programmed as co-directors, and a year later Anouilh ventured out alone as director, arming himself with *Le Songe du critique,* the curtain-raiser for his production of Molière's *Tartuffe* at the Comédie des Champs-Elysées.

Anouilh thought it necessary to fashion a weapon with which to fend off the criticisms that he knew would be forthcoming. *Le*

Songe du critique presents a critic who is raging over the fact that the theater is dying because it is mishandled by directors, the *Tartuffe* presentation he has just attended being a prime example. He bemoans his plight; he cannot write good criticisms because there are no good productions to inspire him. At this point, five characters from *Tartuffe* enter his chamber. The critic, at first frightened, thinks that they will share his feelings of outrage, but they proceed to defend the director's rendition of the play and to condemn the critic for stressing the letter rather than the spirit of Molière. Finally, the critic breaks down in tears and confesses that the reason for his harsh reviews is his desperate loneliness and his dread of having each evening to face a blank sheet of paper which he must cover with words. His personal misery causes him to say wicked things about directors even though he may have enjoyed a play immensely. The critic then dismisses the five characters, declaring with Augustan *noblesse* that he will write a clement review, and a choir of angels sings over his head as the curtain falls, to rise again on Anouilh's production of *Tartuffe*.

Anouilh probably felt more comfortable in the co-director relationship than in the solo undertaking. The following year he again collaborated with Pietri in a highly acclaimed staging of Roger Vitrac's *Victor;* and his three subsequent plays, *La Grotte* (1961), *La Foire d'empoigne* (1962), and *L'Orchestre* (1962), were jointly staged by the playwright and Pietri.

As soon as it was recognized that Anouilh intended quite seriously to devote his efforts to stage directing, he was repeatedly invited to become a member of the French stage directors' union, but Anouilh always declined, in keeping with his conservative socio-economic ideas. That he was against organized labor in all of its forms is manifest in the unsavory tone he bestows on characters in his plays who belong to unions.[16] His spokesman in *L'Hurluberlu* condemns social security systems, and sees no reason for getting sentimental about the idea of the well-being of the masses. For him, the masses are composed of one imbecile added to the next, with nothing sacred about their total.

Anouilh defended his rejection of union membership on the grounds that his enterprises were circumscribed by the fact that the plays he was directing were his own. His alleged answer to the union leaders who were pestering him to join was: "A mother who nurses her child is not necessarily a member of the nursemaids' union," to which critics retorted that Anouilh was a kidnaper, nursing not only his own children, but Vitrac's too.[17]

During the summer of 1963 Anouilh, who had consistently attempted to remain as detached as possible from both Parisian theatrical society and political controversy, nevertheless found himself in a discomforting limelight. While working at the Comédie Française on the production of his own adaptation of Shakespeare's *Richard III*, which was to be a highlight of the national theater's 1963 season, an alleged disagreement with the de Gaulle government brought Anouilh's work to a halt. Offering neither comment nor explanation of the disagreement, Jean Anouilh once again declined to wash French dirty laundry in public.

Literary manifestations of the Anouilh-de Gaulle clash had appeared as early as 1958, with the playwright's pointed references to a conspiring General in *L'Hurluberlu* (not produced until 1959 for reasons of expediency) and with subsequent uncomplimentary allusions to General de Gaulle. In *Le Songe du critique*, Anouilh mocks de Gaulle's Cabinet and notably André Malraux, the Minister for Cultural Affairs, possibly because Malraux was serving the General's designs to kill the spirit of *divertissement* in the French theater. In any case, *Richard III* was produced in 1964—not, however, at the state-run Comédie Française, but at the Théâtre Montparnasse-Gaston Baty, the home of theatrical innovation and progress.

Related to the Anouilh-de Gaulle feud was the rumor circulated in 1963 to the effect that the former had given up playwriting. To an interviewer's query on the matter in September, 1964, Anouilh answered: "Perhaps next year. I feel the spring coiling in me. I want to do something that can't be put on in France, something the government will absolutely forbid." [18]

The spring uncoiled in 1968 in the form of *Le Boulanger, la Boulangère et le Petit Mitron,* an excoriating indictment of bourgeois parents. The play that will redeem Anouilh's political honor still remains to be written, but by breaking his long silence he has abided by his 1959 declaration that "honor, for a playwright, is to be a maker of plays."

CHAPTER 2

General Themes in the Work of Anouilh

THE majority of Jean Anouilh's dramatic works have been grouped under adjectives descriptive of the dominant tone or the distinguishing characteristic of the plays in each category. In plays classified as "black," "pink," "brilliant," "jarring," and "costumed," Anouilh treats an assortment of themes that range from the soul of man to the world of men, from the heroism of the individual to the mediocrity of the masses. Some of the plays are heavy and dismal, some are light and fanciful, but all reveal the author's profound and often painful insight into the human condition.

I The Impurity of Happiness

The "black" and "new black" plays are pessimistic, bitter, and permeated with gloom; they display most clearly Anouilh's lack of faith in humanity and its institutions. His pessimism stems from the realization that neither the so-called joys and comforts of life reserved for the "happy few," nor the invitations to unsavory adventures, promiscuity, and immorality extended to all men, lead to happiness. At the same time, resignation to abject poverty, rigid acceptance of one's role in life, strict morality, and punctilious observance of a code of honor can lead only to tragedy and death.

Purity and love cannot prevail on this earth because of the intrinsic impurity of happiness. Anouilh's heroes and heroines, seeking a happiness known only to themselves, a "purity" of self and an "absolute" love, are faithful in their search even though they know that none is attainable in life. Heroes cannot be "happy"; because they reject *le sale petit bonheur* reserved for the mediocre, they are condemned to a solitude which admits of neither love nor friendship. Their task of finding or creating the *ambiance* in which their truth can thrive is limited to the realms of illusion and death, where real love and purity do exist.

God as well as man forbids the realization of true love on this earth. A cynic in one of the "new black" plays describes a sleeping God who does not disturb lovers, provided that they do not make too much noise: ". . . but what a nose he has, what an extraordinary sense of smell, how he smells the odor of love! And he doesn't like love at all. So then he wakes up and begins to focus on you. And then everything starts jumping, army-style." [1]

The Count in *La Répétition* describes love as putting everything around you into its proper place, causing everything to be peaceful and simple, but, at the same time, as being the most elusive of man's blessings. Camille Desmoulins, Robespierre's friend in *Pauvre Bitos*, begs the revolutionary leader to mitigate his pride and to open his heart: "I admire and still love you, Robespierre. Do you want me to get on my knees to you? Open your heart. Do not remain locked up and snarling in your rigorous prison of logic where we cannot reach you." [2] Camille is the champion of love; Robespierre has him killed.

Becket had inspired the love of the downtrodden masses of Canterbury by continually championing them against the power of the Crown, the rich, and the Normans. Becket and the disciplined, humble men of Sandwich (as opposed to the riotous mobs) are a microcosm of an "ordered world," just as are Joan of Arc and her world of the poor, the ill, the aged, and the wounded. King Henry, although mad with love for Becket, knows only how to buy affection and refuses to love in the way that will allow him to be part of Becket's world.

With Becket, as with all of Anouilh's heroes, offerings of worldly gain are meaningless. In their search for the realization of an ideal far beyond the horizon of the masses, the temptations of the so-called good things in life do not sway the heroic from their perpetual task of refusing mediocrity. Love and happiness that are not pure and absolute are to be avoided at all costs. Antigone's retort to her family's assurances that happiness awaits her because she is young, beautiful, and engaged to be married, is: "You all disgust me with your happiness. With your life that has to be lived at any cost. And that daily ration of good fortune, which suffices as long as you're not too demanding." [3] In words which echo Joan's "I don't want to have a happy ending . . . an ending that never ends,"[4] she rejects Creon's image of a marriage that will permit her to live happily ever after.

The hero's rejection of a love that is less than perfect is incomprehensible to the mediocre masses, for whom "love and marriage" are an integral part of life. Joan of Arc's disappearance from her father's farm to keep her divine appointment provokes her mother's prodding for explanations of the long absence and her father's "Ah! you're losing track of time, now! I hope to God you haven't lost something else that you don't dare mention!"[5] It would be inconceivable for Joan to answer "Saint Michael" to parents such as these. In *Antigone* the uncomprehending Nurse immediately assumes that her charge's absence from the palace in the middle of the night can only be explained by a tryst with a common boy. Again, it would be absurd for Antigone to answer that she had gone to cover the body of her dead brother.

Joan might avoid her father's violent thrashings and be "happier" if only she would try to appear attractive to a village boy who will marry her and thereby ease her father's mind and his blows. She recognizes her father's right to destroy her physically, but maintains her spiritual rights: "Beat me hard; you have the right to. But it's my right to continue to believe and to say no to you."[6] After an especially hard paternal drubbing, she refuses her mother's consolatory offer of an embroidered scarf: "I don't want to look pretty, mommy. . . . I don't want to get married, mother."[7] Later in the play her words express even more clearly her renunciation of happiness and her desire for nonconformity: "I don't want things to turn out all right. . . . I don't want to live your time."[8]

Medea has already experienced marriage: the short, happy union which is soon followed by the inevitable period of noncommunication and which eventually culminates in silence and hatred. Medea's Nurse tells her mistress that "the earth is still full of good things: the sun on the bench at the resting-place, hot soup at noon, the coins you have earned in your hand, the drop of booze that warms your heart before you doze off."[9] Medea, nauseated by her Nurse's mediocrity, banishes her to unheroic realms: "You have said too much, with your carcass, your drop of booze, and your sun shining on your rotten flesh. Get back to your dishes, your broom, your peelings, you and the rest of your race."[10]

Turning toward Corinth, where the people are celebrating boisterously, Medea says: "Something in me is stirring . . . and it says *no* to happiness."[11] Her own children disgust her, for she already sees them as sly, deceitful men who are, worst of all, anxious to live and to be happy. Nowhere in Anouilh's plays does a heroine seek to satisfy her maternal instinct. Children are never portrayed as a delight or a comfort, but rather as tiring, vociferous mini-adults. In one play (*La Répétition*) the author is unsparing: his characters find deaf-mute children perhaps tolerable, but rose bushes preferable.

The acceptance of "happiness" means, for Anouilh's heroes, submersion into the eternal oblivion of conformity, which is the equivalent of vegetation. Jason had formerly been the ideal for whom Medea had sacrificed all. After their marriage his love was lost and that love now repels her. When he tries to save her from the many enemies she has made because of him, she protests: "What are you trying to save? This worn-out skin, this carcass Medea, good for nothing except to drag around in its boredom and its hatred? A little bread and a house somewhere, and she'll grow old in silence until nobody mentions her name any more, right?"[12] In the same way Electra, describing Aegisthus' and Clytemnestra's marriage as a slow process of watching the approach of old age, the onset of coldness, lack of desire and ultimately hatred, exclaims sardonically: "Oh, indissoluble sanctity of marriage!"[13]

It is in the "jarring" plays that Anouilh expounds most discordantly upon the subjects of life and love, marriage and children. The plays end on a displeasing, disconcerting note, expressing a total cynicism regarding the possibility of love existing between a man and a woman. Although based upon the solid foundation of money, even the marriages of the wealthy are no happier. What the poor heroes fear as the influence of money on love, the rich know and live as a daily routine: boredom, hostility, hatred, deception, hypocrisies of all kinds. Everything that Frantz (the hero of Anouilh's first play, *L'Hermine*) predicted if he were to marry, is illustrated in the later plays, where the ugliness and sordidness of married life become a self-fulfilling prophecy. No truly happy couple is portrayed in any of the plays, and whatever pleasure might have existed in the premarital state is soon destroyed by marriage.

Anouilh has described marriage as a chemical experiment in

which "a mixture at first bubbles and sparkles; then happiness volatilizes, leaving in the retort nothing but a big gray lump of [marital] obligations." [14] The grotesque Madame Alexandra (in *Colombe*) reveals what the excitement over marriage is all about: she has had seven marital experiences, with husbands ranging from a neo-Nero to a devourer of live rats, and has even married one of her husbands twice—once after his mother's and once after his father's death—not to console him, but to help him squander his millions. Anouilh's "Jezabel" is described by her husband as the "sweetest, frailest young bride imaginable, for whom two years sufficed to become a shrew." [15] The stock figure of General Saint-Pé (in *Ardèle, La Valse des Toréadors,* and *L'Hurluberlu*) is the symbol of the pathetic, disillusioned, humiliated, and unheroic married man.

II *Friendship-Love*

If, for Anouilh, marriage is not the ideal relationship between two human beings, friendship-love can be. As long as Colombe and Julien, a young couple in love, are "allies," as long as Jason and Medea are "brother and sister," as long as Becket and King Henry are "companions," the basis for happy union exists. The moment that conformity to social patterns is introduced, however, the ideal friendship-love dies.

This friendship-love is a "pure" relationship and, as such, can only thrive among "pure" individuals. According to Anouilh, however, every individual is escorted by his past, his family, his education, and his habits, all of which superimpose their traits upon the original pure being. If persons were left alone, then isolated purity and love could exist, but in the world as we know it antagonisms constantly arise between memories of past formation and present conditions. Tragedy is linked with the impossibility of shedding one's sordid past and with the quandary caused by the visualization of an identity that will endear the hero to a society which at the same time victimizes him by smearing his sacred countenance. "Rosiness" and "brilliance" are linked with the ability of the hero to defy society and to create absolute standards for himself despite the relativity of "truth." [16]

III *Sincerity*

Although the hero strives constantly to remain true to himself
and to act accordingly, Anouilh views sincerity as impracticable in
a world which seeks either to use honesty as a stratagem or to
destroy it. In many plays the hero is subjected to anti-sincerity
brainwashings that range from starvation diets to hard labor and
thrashings, yet the hero refuses to assume the artificial airs that
society tries to impose upon him.

In the nineteenth century Thomas Carlyle prophesied that the
world would once more become a *sincere,* believing world with
many heroes in it, and that it would then (and only then) be a
victorious world. His thought is the credo of Anouilh's heroic figures who are true to themselves, convinced that sincerity is their
only salvation. They are isolated in their contemporary world, a
world which is divided and convulsed with insincerity, which em-
ploys tactics stronger than its beliefs, has no heroes, and is con-
sumed with self-doubt. Nevertheless, the heroes persist in their
sincerity and fidelity, for that is their way of loving. The impossibility of their fulfilling their love in an uncomprehending and in-
sincere world is their challenge.

The hero remains his true self within himself, but the futility of
his challenge, the conflict between his ideal and the hypocrisy of a
sordid reality, leads him quite logically to a decision to escape his
milieu. In the *pièces noires* the antagonism between the "pure"
hero and perverted society results in either actual or symbolic
death or in insanity as a form of escape. In the *pièces roses* and
the *pièces brillantes*[17] escape takes the form of either the creation
of an illusion that triumphs over reality or a refuge in one's multiple personalities.

Anouilh is deeply concerned with this idea of the multiplicity
and mutability of the human personality, and with the realization
that man cannot be reduced to a unity that will afford him inner
peace and contentment. He is aware of the relativity of human
sentiments and emotions to social, sociological, and economic conditions, and the disturbing feelings of disunity that result from the
conflict between them. Perhaps the most forceful example the author has given us of a heroine for whom changing human opinions
have no significance is Joan of Arc, who, in the face of the relative

truths of her parents, the people of France, and her executioners, remains a symbol of absolute truth.

IV The Race of the Rich and the Race of the Poor

Another predominant theme in Anouilh's plays is that of the implacable opposition and eternal irreconcilability of the "race" of the rich and the "race" of the poor, and the necessity for both races to accept segregation. The poor heroes are fully aware of the reality of their poverty. While the rich antagonists are oblivious to the "unreal" world of the poor, they fear at the same time an invasion from lower space.

In an early play (*L'Hermine*), the hero, believing that money could secure love, was driven to committing murder before discovering that wealth and happiness are unrelated. In a later play (*La Sauvage*) the impoverished heroine understands that it is not lack of money that prevents the lasting union of herself and her wealthy lover, but rather the fact that their two worlds can never coalesce. She speaks of a "lost dog wandering about somewhere, which prevents me from ever being happy." [18] The lost dog (symbolic of her poverty and her sordid past) has taken the place of money in preventing happiness.

The vile "luggage" of their past prevents the poor from ever making a transition into the race of the rich. The impenetrable barrier between the two races is vividly illustrated by the two-level stage décor of *La Grotte*: on the lower kitchen level writhes the poor domestic help; on the upper level revel the rich Count and Countess. All of Anouilh's characters line up on one level or the other: commoners bearing the names of Isabelle, Amanda, Frantz, Thérèse, Lucile, Jeannette, etc. are all of the poor race; the stock Princes, Duchesses, Counts, Countesses and Ladies are their rich counterparts. The poor suffer abuse, the physical hardships of immorality, disease, unwanted children, etc.; the rich condone sexual promiscuity with members of their own class, but not with members of the lower class because, according to Anouilh, bastard sons of noblemen turn sour later in life and foment revolutions.

In *Le Songe du critique* Anouilh has described (through the character Tartuffe) his typical hero of the "poor race":

> There he is—the poor man, always quick and on his guard,
> The poor, unhappy man, the cheating bastard, spurned
> and scarred,
> Tired of the rich, with all their barriers and boulders.
> He lives to take his vengeance, for in order to be fed
> He must conceal his bitterness and scorn, and smile
> instead—
> The poor man, with his clumsiness to weigh upon his
> shoulders.[19]

Although the members of the poor race refer to themselves as stupid, dirty, tactless, cuckolded and cynical, they insist upon remaining true to themselves and their concept of honor. They cannot afford to do otherwise. Rather than prostrate themselves hypocritically to earn enough to "graze twice a day like donkeys," impoverished heroes choose to behave in a way judged as stupid by society's standards. Heroines, refusing orchids, champagne, and furs, will request baser beverages and seek instead the warmth of a hand in their revolt against hypocrisy.

Anouilh's distinction between the heroic and the mediocre is also explained in terms of the "poor" and the "rich" races. Of the two, it is the poor race that fathers heroes, not the wealthy or the nobility. The lower class produces geniuses, while the upper class spends its life taking futility seriously. By the very rottenness of family life among the wealthy, with its inanity, its *ménages à trois* or *à quatre,* its hypocrisy, and its alcoholism, the growth of heroism and genius is stunted.

Within the poor race itself, Anouilh distinguishes between the happy and the unhappy, the mediocre and the heroic. He describes the former as "an exploding, fertile race, a flabby mass of dough that eats its sausage, bears children, uses its tools, counts its *sous,* year after year, in spite of epidemics and wars, until old age catches up with it; people living life, everyday people, people it's hard to imagine as dead." The latter he describes as "the noble ones, the heroes. Those whom you can easily imagine stretched out dead, pale, with a bullet hole in the head— . . . the cream of the crop." [20]

Anouilh conceives of the "flabby masses of dough" throughout the centuries as Hobbes's *homo lupus hominem*—wolves against wolves. They take the form of the Rouen mob awaiting the spectacle of the burning of Joan of Arc; the Paris mob howling at the foot of the guillotine during the Revolution; the spitting, stench-ing Thebes mob described in *Antigone,* with its thousand arms and its thousand faces, but with its one indistinguishable expres-sion of mockery and laughter.

The heroes look disdainfully upon the mediocrity of those who inhabit the realms of superficiality, conformity, and weakness; this majority is analogous with the "rich race" in that it masks truths and is afraid to face absolutes. Rather than daring to dream of something better, the mediocre take refuge in their petty mala-dies, their banalities, and their stomachs. The members of the he-roic race seek answers to metaphysical questions and are eternally dissatisfied with themselves, for they know what they could have become had the circumstances been different; they scorn society's masks and hypocrisies and life itself, refusing to make any com-promise which might prevent the realization of their true selves. Their conscience and concept of order, clearly conceived and stated, form the sharp dividing line between the rigorous de-mands of honor and the mediocre satisfactions of the masses.

V   *Honor*

Anouilh's heroes love honor not for honor's sake, but for the sake of an *idea of honor* which they have created for themselves. When, for example, King Henry asks for Becket's mistress, Becket offers her with the words, "My honor leaves much to be de-sired," [21] revealing that Becket has not yet found the idea of honor for which he will die; he has not chosen the defense of woman's honor as his ennobling task, nor the soldier's honor, which would require him to conquer, nor English honor, which would demand that he defend the honor of the King. It is only later in the play that he will choose to defend the concept of God's honor invoked by the title that will be bestowed upon him, that of Archbishop. The pursuit of honor is strengthened not by God, but by Becket's esthetic sense of how an Archbishop should defend God's honor. While honor, for Anouilh's anti-heroes, is something to be remembered and forgotten at will, to be bought and sold, soiled and washed, the hero's idea of honor can be neither impro-vised nor defiled by compromise.

The concept of an honor to be defended unto death is basic to Anouilh's plays. The theme, which recurs clearly and frequently, is linked to the playwright's championing of nonconformity, purity, and refusal to compromise. For Anouilh, those who defend wealth and material possessions cannot defend a concept of honor. A truly sorry figure, for example, is King Charles of France in *L'Alouette,* who has neither wealth, nor courage, nor anyone to defend his person, much less his title. For this pusillanimous king, the concept of honor is nonexistent.

VI *Absurd Duty*

The hero's refusal to betray his intransigent race and his search for a purity that transcends any relationship of compromise are best illustrated in the "costumed" plays, which present heroic, historic, or legendary figures. Their duty is to remain loyal to their race, regardless of how absurd or grotesque their role may be.

The sole commandment of Anouilh's "insolent breed" of heroes is to do what has to be done, when it has to be done, and to do it wholeheartedly and completely even though it is unpleasant and difficult; this maxim would allow them to create an historically ordered world were it not for the mediocre race.[22] Morality may be for external use only, but once a role in life is assigned it cannot be doffed. Stated negatively, in Becket's words, "the only thing that is immoral is . . . not doing what is necessary when it is necessary." [23] To Henry's pleas for logic, Becket retorts: "That's not necessary, my King. The only thing necessary is to do, absurdly, what has been assigned to you, and carry it through to the end." [24] Cauchon, the churchman who is somewhat more humane than the Inquisitor in *L'Alouette,* pleads with Joan of Arc: "Joan, try to understand that there is something absurd about your refusal." [25] Antigone persistently tells Creon that she must return to her brother's grave to replace the earth that the guards have removed. Creon replies: "You will return to perform such an absurd gesture again? . . . Even if you should succeed in covering the grave again, you know very well that we will uncover the cadaver. So what are you accomplishing except covering your fingernails with blood and getting yourself hanged?" Antigone answers: "Nothing but that, I know. But at least I can do that. And everyone must do whatever he can do." [26]

The "insolent ones" are confident that God or the gods favor them and will grant them sufficient time in which to accomplish with appropriate dignity their absurd duty. Antigone will have performed the funeral rites for her dead brother with her tiny, rusty spade, and Becket will go to his death with every little hook and eye in his intricate robe properly attached. It is all a matter of esthetics—not fear of worldly punishment or fear of God. Anouilh's heroes find lies repugnant, deception indecent, compromise inelegant; they insist upon being esthetically "pure," upon playing their role down to the last detail. Becket achieves an absolute triumph when he proclaims that "the honor of God . . . has permitted that I be killed in my Primatial Church. That is the only decent place for me." [27]

Anouilh's hero is willing to adopt the commandment to do what has to be done even though it may be absurd because he has been unable to find a solid truth in society, one upon which he can base his definition of self and his actions. The roots of his tragedy lie in the disjointed relations between himself and other men: Becket is unable to see King Henry as his true prince; Antigone cannot accept Creon as her true authority; Frenchmen kill their heroes and then seek to destroy each other in blood.

Medea could be happy in a world without Jason (who symbolizes compromise), but she knows that the world contains both Jason and herself, and, therefore, the seeds of conflict. She will have to oppose him unarmed in a losing battle, because he is of the "rich" race. She cries out to him: "Race of Abel, race of the just, race of the rich, how calmly you speak. It must be good to have the gods on your side and the police, too." [28] The serenity of the mediocre race is denied the frenzied heroes and heroines who obstreperously reject the maxim that physical, political, and military might makes right.

Antigone's position, vis-à-vis a king who demands compromise, is identical to that of Medea. Antigone loves both life and her fiancé Haemon, but will nevertheless perform the burial rites for her brother in the face of certain death. Becket, as soon as he is named Archbishop of Canterbury, begins defending God's honor against the honor of the kingdom, although bitterly reproaching God with the words: "How difficult you make everything and how heavy is your honor!" [29]

Anouilh's heroes reject all concepts of compromise and conformity. In the hero's world every action or sentiment of honor is starkly delineated and labeled; there is no gray area offering refuge and the opportunity to avoid justification of one's life. While the heroic refuse to accept the definition of happiness proffered by the mediocre, the mediocre, in turn, can understand neither what it is that the heroes are seeking, nor why they absent themselves both physically and mentally from the routine and accepted way of life.

The life span of the mediocre man is, for Anouilh's heroes and heroines, nothing but an endless and ugly vegetation. So powerful is their scorn of life's *sale espoir* that, just as Joan of Arc is about to recant and Antigone about to accede to her uncle's reasoning, the reminders of Warwick and Creon, respectively, are enough for the heroines once again to prefer death to an act of compromise.

The vicarious experience of "living" makes the heroic even more determined, at the crucial and decisive moment, to refuse to understand, to refuse to be "reasonable." "Moi, je ne veux comprendre," is Antigone's rejoinder throughout the play, and it is echoed in other plays by heroines who refuse to be "reasonable" by conforming to society's norms. Refusal to "live," to "grow up and understand," is a dominant theme in Anouilh's theater, but the desire to remain childlike, contrary to the suggestion of one critic,[30] is not a form of desire for regression. It is, rather, a reasoned and deliberate decision not to conform when an ideal or a concept of honor is threatened.

Because of the paucity of nonconformists who refuse to understand, the world will never be saved. As the General in *L'Hurluberlu* states: "We must give up trying to understand. . . . People have been trying too long to understand. That's why nothing is going right any more. If the world is to be saved, it will be saved by imbeciles!"[31] Although the ridiculous character Ledadu responds with "Present, General," thus making the scene comic, Anouilh's basic idea is nevertheless maintained. Ledadu is not an "imbecile" by Anouilh's definition, because he really is one. Anouilh's imbeciles are heroes who have accepted a concept of duty that is seemingly absurd; imbecility is synonymous with acceptance of absurdity.

Persons in power attempt unsuccessfully to dissuade extremists from their nonconformity by demonstrating the absurdity of their ideal. Creon tries to destroy Antigone's illusions by smearing the image in her mind of her brother Polynices and revealing that it may even be Eteocles' body that she has buried instead. Her sister Ismene tries to dissuade her from covering the body, arguing that he was not a good brother. Antigone, however, stands firm:

"What do I care about your politics, your necessities, your miserable stories. I can still say 'no' . . . and I am sole judge." [32] The concept of an absurd duty to be fulfilled can be judged only by a superior race of "imbeciles."

Cauchon, the Bishop of Beauvais, in an attempt to destroy the will of the imprisoned Joan of Arc, tells her that all of her good soldiers have abandoned her and, weary of war, have fled Rouen. Even La Hire, her closest companion in battle, has hired himself out as a mercenary, she is told, but higher voices also speak to Joan, and she persists in her heroism. The Count in *La Répétition* is defamed by a drunken noble who, in league with the Countess, attempts to disabuse Lucile, who cherishes the Count and her own illusions about him. The heroine obstinately refuses to leave the Château, where she has found the ideal that she had been seeking, and persists in believing in the superiority of the Count despite most convincing evidence of his flightiness.

The dialogue in *Pauvre Bitos* between the Jesuit Schoolmaster and the young, nonconforming Robespierre illustrates a similar confrontation: "(Schoolmaster:) Your mind is not sufficiently respectful. There is something rigid in your mind that disturbs me. . . . (Robespierre:) Yes, Father. (Schoolmaster:) You say yes, and there is something in your mind that says no. We shall punish you until your mind says yes." [33] The Schoolmaster's whippings succeed only in strengthening Robespierre's will to resist and ultimately to realize his personal ambitions.

VII *Acceptance of Death*

Although Anouilh's heroes will accept death, if necessary, in order to fulfill their concept of duty, they nevertheless love life and cling to it humbly and sentimentally. Unabashed in seeking ways to lessen their fear, they are not at all like Corneille's classical protagonists, who die without openly expressing their innermost feelings. The Prologue in *Antigone* tells us that, as the heroine sits silently on the stage, she thinks about the fact that she is going to die, that she is young and that she would have liked to live, but that there is no changing the role that she must play. Later in the play the following exchange takes place between Antigone and her sister: "(Ismene:) I don't want to die. (Antigone:) I too would have liked not to die. . . . (Ismene:) I'm not very courageous, you know. (Antigone:) Neither am I. But what difference does it make?" [34] An almost identical scene is to be found in *Médée:* "(Nurse:) I am old, I don't want to die. (Medea:) I too . . . would have liked to live." [35]

Joan of Arc, when asked by Cauchon whether she is afraid to die, admits that she is afraid but that it makes no difference. Orestes is asked by Electra whether he is afraid to die. His answer is "Do it quickly," even though he is perfectly calm when he is called out of his palace to die. Antigone and Medea also seek a swift death. Medea pours out her emotions to her Nurse, expressing her dread of physical pain; for her, as for Antigone, physical contact with her Nurse (despite her mediocrity) will help to calm her fears. Joan of Arc shares with King Charles her method for eliminating fear: have a tremendously big fear all at once, and then cast off all traces of it as you plunge into battle.

Frantz (in *L'Hermine*) personifies fear as a dog about to attack, explaining that it is necessary to grip it until it falls to the ground, then take it and hold it against your own body, mouth to mouth, until your hair stands up straight and your teeth chatter; then you will have entered into the realm of silence and shadow, where you can sleep with a corpse without fear. For Jeannette (in *Roméo et Jeannette*) and for General Saint-Pé, a little piece of red blotting paper baptized "*mininistatfia*," chewed at the appropriate moment, gives strength and conquers all fears.

Invariably, the heroes must ultimately bear their emotions and fears alone. They stand firm in the full knowledge that they have been abandoned by all and that, in the end, society will destroy them. Antigone, after Ismene's renunciation of her part in the burial of Polynices, realizes that it is up to her alone to defy Creon's edict. Creon, as the author of that edict, is also alone, but he can never reach the stature of the heroine who has made no compromise with life. Electra and Medea are solitary, inaccessible heroines, abandoned by gods and men.

Anouilh's description of Joan of Arc is suited also to his other heroes and heroines: "Joan continues . . . with that curious mixture of humility and insolence, of grandeur and common sense, even up to the stake; . . . it is in this solitude, in this silence of an absent God, in this deprivation and this bestial misery, that the man who continues to hold his head high is great. Great and alone." [36] Heroic defenders of honor create discomfort in others. King Louis, although regretful that a man as extraordinary as

Becket was not born on his side of the Channel, nevertheless reveals his awareness that Becket might have caused him trouble, and is relieved that the hero will return to England to meet his doom.

Like Joan of Arc, Anouilh's heroes are "little skylark[s] immobile against the sun, being shot at" [37]—an image which greatly disturbs those who have power but not glory. The Inquisitor in *L'Alouette*, for example, explains that the smaller, the frailer, the more tender, the *purer* the enemy, the more formidable he is. When Creon is told that it was a child who covered the grave of Polynices, he muses over the dialogue which he anticipates between himself and the pale, defiant rebel, knowing well that haughty contempt awaits him.

Describing George Bernard Shaw's Joan of Arc, Harold Clurman has written: "She has to be stopped, done away with, because like all fanatically persistent moralists, she is a pest, a threat, unbearable to the ordinary. . . . Though she wins in history, she must lose in her person. She herself recognizes this, but cannot and does not wish to curb her force and fail her fate." [38] Only when the fragile little "enemies" of the Church or of the State are removed from the scene does stability again reign, but only temporarily, until the next hero arises. After each new hero falls under the Inquisition, or the guillotine, or, more recently, firing squads, silent calm descends upon the State, until the next gunshots fired at a skylark are heard.

VIII *The Pseudo-Hero*

In some of his later plays, Anouilh seems to have conceived of a modified hero, less rigid in his refusal to compromise. This "pseudo-hero" type acts out his part in a gray area between duty and compromise. He is seen in King Henry Plantagenet (*Becket*, 1959) and in the Count (*La Grotte*, 1961), but is best embodied in the character of General Saint-Pé (*Ardèle*, 1949; *La Valse des Toréadors*, 1952; *L'Hurluberlu*, 1959), who seems to represent a stage of Anouilh's own life and conscience.

The pseudo-hero is a *réactionnaire amoureux* (the subtitle of *L'Hurluberlu*), a two-faced marionette thirsting for love, pining for "the good old days," playing out his hatred, his desire for vengeance, his fear of the world, his awareness of his own ugliness, and his embarrassment in the presence of women. Although this type seems to retain in his conscience the concept of absolute standards, in his actions he suppresses conscience and vacillates between rigidity and compromise. When he is rigid, he is ridiculous; when he compromises, he is unhappy.

The earlier heroes were faced with this same dilemma, and their decision was to avenge themselves. Electra had learned hatred all by herself, and, together with Orestes, she enacted it unflinchingly. Their unhappiness stemmed from their mother's infidelity and the assassination of their father, who had to be avenged, just as Antigone had to avenge her brother and Medea had to avenge herself. The difference between these heroes and the pseudo-heroes, however, is that they themselves are the sole judge of their actions. Their concept of duty and honor is inflexible, and involves the sacrifice of life itself; none of the other characters in the plays inspire pity for them or excuse them.

These early heroes are literally extracted from the mediocre masses, while the later hero is pitifully manipulated and victimized; the greatest weakness of his personality has been found and exploited by society. The middle-aged Saint-Pé, the congenial Count in *Ardèle* and *La Répétition*, the conscience-ridden but otherwise revolting Ornifle and the cruel Bitos, redeemed only by his pitifulness, are humanity's whipping boys. If they momentarily rise to great heights, it is only to intensify their groveling.

The pseudo-hero has no absolute standards; he simply has a conscience that bothers him whenever he strays from his duty, as he frequently enjoys doing. Conscience stirs and fills a void in the heart of poor old Saint-Pé, who refuses to abandon his demented wife even though he cherishes and desires another woman; that conscience, however, is not sufficiently strong to permit him to discontinue his trysts with his true love. The conscience in the Count's household is Ardèle, his hunchbacked sister, to whose reasoning and logic he is highly susceptible, but conscience loses at the end of the tragic play.

Conscience in *Ornifle* is embodied in a blatantly conspicuous character, Mademoiselle Supo. Ornifle is constantly made aware of her presence, even though he tries to banish her from his sight and to deny the reality of her person. He tells Supo: "Don't keep comparing yourself with my conscience. My conscience is a charming, well-behaved young lady. I have trained her not to eavesdrop. My conscience never asks me what I'm doing." [39]

As in the early plays, the world of some of Anouilh's later plays is one for men—not heroes. The pseudo-hero, like the hero, is resigned to the fact that his own life, as well as the lives of others, is meaningless. The author appears to have momentarily settled for the relativity of truth and seems less determined to abide by absolutes alone. With his mellower philosophy Anouilh depicts "little" men struggling to maintain a place in the sun—nothing more noble or heroic or grandiose than that. Even historical giants such as Napoleon and Louis XVIII are doing nothing more in *La Foire d'empoigne* (1962) than playing a petty game of grab, catching as catch can, unmindful of their unheroic demeanor.

Whether Anouilh's change of heart is due to his chagrin at the performance of an uncompromising and rigid leader of the French government remains problematical. Former Premier Georges Pompidou, in a 1967 broadcast, said that the choice for France was between Gaullist stability and "disorder and confusion," claiming that only the Gaullists could make the era perfect "because we are united." Pompidou's phrases sound curiously like the scenario of an Anouilh play. Perhaps the present-day situation in France will provide the dramatist with a Hegelian synthesis that will resolve the conflict between his thesis of the rigid hero and his antithesis of the compromising hero.

The scope of Anouilh's work is vast. His thoughts, many in the form of maxims, are on a variety of subjects too sweeping to catalog. Most important to remember is his vision of a hero—usually rigid, sometimes plastic—against the backdrop of a corrupt society. Through his heroes, the solitary Anouilh satisfies his pressing need to express and reveal himself; it is as though he himself were standing on the stage before us, speaking harshly and impulsively, seeking not pity, but recognition of ourselves as the cause of his torment. We are the ones who perpetrate society's corruption and injustices; we are the ones who stifle the pure instincts of youth and idealism; we are the ones who debase professions and careers by our venality and our brutality. We have created the horror that surrounds us and that makes us grow old without having understood the symbolism of the immobile skylark.

CHAPTER 3

Pièces noires *and* Nouvelles pièces noires

I *L'Hermine and Jézabel*

ANOUILH'S very first *pièces noires, L'Hermine* and *Jézabel,* (both written in 1932), are brutal, naturalist melodramas. *L'Hermine* presents a solitary young man, comparable in some ways to Raskolnikov in *Crime and Punishment,* who commits a violent murder in the belief that money alone will secure his happiness. Anouilh's hero Frantz is, in a sense, a reflection of the author himself: his youth, spent in poverty, has been petty and disgusting.

Frantz refuses to expose his young fiancée Monime, the niece of a Duchess, to that poverty; he would prefer to marry her off himself to a wealthy man. He reveals to his confidant Philippe that he cannot be content, as is Philippe, with earning a monthly pittance working for a newspaper; he must have large sums of money to realize his dream of love and happiness. Until he succeeds, Frantz chooses to live alone, rejecting friendship, facile relations with women, and café conversation with acquaintances. Following the initial failure of a business venture, Frantz has, for two years, been attempting to raise money by writing, but his endeavors have been fruitless. Now, at the age of twenty-five, he feels that his ideas, his perseverance, and he himself are dead.

At the end of Act II, Frantz receives a telegram from Bentz, a wealthy entrepreneur to whom the hero had sold his business at a loss, offering him a job at 2,000 francs per month. Cynically, he muses that the salary would be just enough to cover Monime's monthly wardrobe expenses. Frantz sees no alternative but the murder of the Duchess, with his fiancée's consequent inheritance of her fortune. He contemplates his crime at length, divulges his intentions to Monime, and, after a struggle to overcome their fears, he finally perpetrates the brutal murder. Frantz is now marked by his *"mains sales."* Monime recoils from his bloody hands and accuses him of killing for her money. He turns away from her, bitterly resigning himself to the fact that she is of the "good race" and he of the "odious race"; that his attempt to find nonexistent love and friendship has been pointless. With the familiar words of the intransigent hero in the face of an absurd, self-conceived duty, "I am ridiculous. I am absolutely ridiculous," Frantz surrenders himself to the police.

Jézabel (Anouilh gives the shameless and dissolute anti-heroine the name of the notorious wife of Ahab, King of Israel) portrays a woman completely unexalted in her criminality. Through her persistently immoral behavior she denies her son Marc any happiness that would be made possible by a change in her way of life. Marc, like Frantz, would like to give the young woman he loves (Jacqueline) a beautiful married life worthy of the respect and admiration of all, but his mother, the "Jezabel" of the title, is a fat, lazy alcoholic and the mistress of Jacqueline's father's chauffeur, and his father is a vulgar man with a propensity for chasing maids. Marc pleads with his parents to reform, and though he dreams of an ideal father and mother who would allow him to be happy, no amount of dreaming can change the mediocre race or allow Marc to "shed his past."

The chauffeur, threatened with imprisonment if he does not return the 5,000 francs he has stolen from his employer, forces his mistress to obtain the money for him. "Jezabel" goes on her knees to her son in the hope that her loneliness and wretchedness will evoke in him some pity, but Marc refuses his mother the money, as had his father before him. In desperation "Jezabel" knowingly serves poison mushrooms to her husband; her crime is of no avail, however, for the chauffeur deserts her. Marc's initial reaction is to leave home, to erase all traces of his past and to become "an orphan without memories"; but his mother has now become such an abject, pitiful figure that Marc suddenly feels "responsible" for her and for all that she symbolizes: we once again see "the lost dog wandering about somewhere," preventing the hero from ever finding happiness. Although totally innocent, Marc implicates himself in his mother's crime in order to frighten away his beloved Jacqueline, for he knows that she does not belong in his world.

The turning point in the play is the moment "Jezabel" reveals the murder to her son: her very helplessness now challenges Marc

to defend her, rather than be ashamed of her. His father's relatives try to disabuse him by telling him how, when he was still a
young child, she neglected him, leaving him to his father's care.
They urge him to abandon this evil woman now that his father is
dead, and it is, perhaps, their very efforts to persuade him that
prompt Marc to refuse to leave his mother. He persists in remaining with her, as Antigone persists in covering her brother's body
even though her family has revealed to her his unwholesome nature.

After confessing her crime to her son, "Jezabel" suddenly ages.
Her hair turns gray. She begs Marc to understand her loneliness
and to hold her in his arms as though she were a child. She is
frightened to remain alone now that her husband is dead and the
chauffeur has left her, and she entreats her son to stay with her.
"Jezabel" has now become the mother-figure that Marc has always
wanted her to be, but this is her symbolic death, for she lived in
the illusion of being able to hold a lover. Her illusion is now destroyed, and she is left with no memories of even a moment of joy
in her love life.

"Jezabel" is a pathetic figure indeed as she explains to her son
why she has taken so many lovers into her life; she was seeking
joy and love, attempting to escape a man who had for her become
a corpse: "I had to get away from him, I had to hear another
voice, feel other arms, living flesh close to mine, flesh that
laughed, suffered, spoke, spent its money—stirred, in a word. . . .
Can't you understand that I was a dead woman wanting desperately to touch trees, animals, warm stones?" [1] Marc does understand that her life had been deprived of joy by his father, that she
had never found love, that she might have devoted her life to her
son, been beautiful just for him, if only he had not become a man,
changing from a pure and innocent child in her arms into someone with whom she could no longer play and communicate. From
the moment he became a man, her husband's lips were tight when
he kissed her, for he had become serious, but he became this way
because he had seen his wife with another man. Once again we
are presented with Anouilh's self-fulfilling prophesy of unhappiness in marriage.

This feeling of wanting to be a child haunts Marc and induces
him to bring Jacqueline into his home: his mother makes him feel
old and sad, while Jacqueline fills him with purity, innocence, and

serenity. "Jezabel," ugly, old, and monstrous, refuses to see Jacqueline, refuses to have her in her home, for she fears that Jacqueline will be able to dissipate the very sordidness that binds her and her son.

The denouement of the play is Jacqueline's attempt, in her idealistic yet sincere belief that the poor, the humble, and the meek shall inherit the earth, to persuade Marc to free himself from his corrosive environment: "You are of another race. Luxury, money, glory, which mean nothing in the hands of others, are reserved for you." [2] She offers to make Marc happy by wiping away all of the anguish and corruption revealed in his face, but Marc responds by forcing his already drunken mother to drink in Jacqueline's presence and then roughly expelling his beloved from his home. Obstinately refusing to understand Jacqueline's love and gentleness, her pity and invitation to happiness, he clings desperately to the squalor that links him to his mother.

When Jacqueline is gone, "Jezabel," victorious and no longer "alone," turns to her son, inviting him to wallow in the filth of their circumscribed world. She will serve her son hand and foot, and Georgette the maid (once she has been paid 500 francs to keep the secret of the poison mushrooms) will be available to satisfy his every desire. Marc, however, dashes out, mad with rage and suffering; the glimpse of purity provided by Jacqueline will prevent him from remaining with "Jezabel."

II La Sauvage

La Sauvage (written in 1934 but first presented in 1938) is in many ways similar to *Jézabel*. Thérèse Tarde, *"la sauvage"* whose sordid life is evoked in relentless detail, is a member of a family of poor, debased café musicians. She is loved by Florent, a wealthy and famous pianist who offers her (as Jacqueline offered Marc in *Jézabel*) marriage, happiness, and forgetfulness of things past. Although Thérèse loves Florent, she foresees the impossibility of transition into the new and respectable milieu that he offers her.

After much hesitation, Thérèse agrees to the engagement and submits to the fittings for her elaborate wedding gown, the symbol of a new life divorced from her past. A few days spent with Florent's family in their sumptuous surroundings, however, convince Thérèse that even her fierce longing for happiness cannot overpower the inexorable grip of her past life. She is obsessed by the vulgarity and pathetic sordidness of her family and her environment and cannot, hypocritically, turn away from them.

Thérèse schemes systematically to break the engagement by summoning her boorish father to Florent's mansion and inciting him, through drink, to display his obscene vulgarity (a similar scene occurs in *Jézabel*), by persuading her fellow musician to write an anonymous letter to Florent warning him against the marriage, and by bribing Jeannette to appear at Florent's home and announce that Thérèse has been the mistress of Gosta, her mother's lover. It is Gosta's appearance on the scene, armed and prepared to take vengeance on Florent after having mercilessly beaten Thérèse's mother, that convinces the heroine that she must return to her original milieu. Thérèse leaves Florent and advances determinedly toward her fixed destiny of unhappiness and corruption, carrying on her back the onerous bundle of her past, "very small, hard and lucid, to be bruised everywhere by the world." [3] Meanwhile, her father (with an attitude reminiscent of the mercenary Georgette in *Jézabel*) worries aloud about his expenses for train fare and a ticking taximeter.

The scene in *La Sauvage* that clearly separates the "races" is the one in which Florent, in a symbolic gesture, throws his thick wads of money upon the ground so that Thérèse may love him not for his money but for himself alone. The heroine, having initially expressed contempt for wealth, is nevertheless true to herself and her race and cannot pretend to wear the mask of hypocrisy: she falls to her knees and gathers up the bills to demonstrate her allegiance to the "race of the poor."

Florent, who is sweetness and consideration personified, is unable to convince Thérèse of his genuine desire to marry her. He poetically introduces his mansion and all of its luxuries individually to her so that she may know them better; although she wilfully responds with vulgarities, Florent persists in his kindness, and just at the moment that Thérèse is about to succumb to Florent's gentleness her father enters, a ludicrous figure in his wedding suit. His appearance saves her from "compromising" herself, in a scene that recalls Antigone's and Joan of Arc's imminent accession to "reasonable" authority until the mention of "happiness" causes them to about-face.[4] Thérèse turns away from Florent (just as Marc spurned Jacqueline) and returns to her father's world with the words: "Ah! we go well together, papa. We understand each other, don't we? We aren't ashamed of each other, we're both of the same race, right?" [5]

At this point in the play Hartmann, an intermediate character who seems to be Anouilh's spokesman, attempts to reconcile the lovers by explaining both sides of the picture to Florent. Hartmann agrees with Thérèse that Florent has had too much good luck in life: he is like a king to whom everything has been given in profusion, and so he must accept, as must all kings, being somewhat of a stranger on earth. When Florent protests that he truly loves Thérèse, Hartmann replies: "That's just where you haven't played the game. Kings must not love anything but their joy." [6] Hartmann admits that, despite his initial contempt of Florent, he is now resigned to him and would like to help him.

Thérèse, once again yielding to her love for Florent, uncovers her soul to Hartmann. She reveals her sincere desire to understand the world of the rich. In her youth she had imagined that she would understand when she was older, that she would be able to use all of her strength to revolt against her own world. Now she is mature and trying desperately to understand that other world; she has an almost puerile eagerness to know how the rich act and think. As her wedding gown is being fitted, she learns from Florent's aunt and sister the concept of "working": jobs in their uncle's bank with long vacations, the problem of finding dresses that can be worn both to "work" and to cocktails and the theater afterwards. We almost know by now that Thérèse will never be able to understand the world of the rich and that she will ultimately leave Florent and never again return. Hartmann's words confirm our suspicions: "I am sure that it has already begun to envelop you, to bring you to life, this filthy happiness." [7]

The heroine is faced with the concept of *"le sale petit bonheur"* [8] and she derisively rejects it. Revolt stirs within her; she cries out that she simply does not want to understand certain things, that she will not be domesticated, and that she will not be tricked into looking only at the agreeable things in life, into employing the technique, used by the happy few to stay young, happy, and rich, of disregarding all unpleasant realities. When, finally, Thérèse's father returns to warn Florent of Gosta's malevolent intention, Thérèse envisions all the people of her past, as though banded together to receive her into their midst and thus preventing her from making any compromise with the rich.

Thérèse, who can reach no comprehension of Florent and his "race," can understand clearly Gosta's despair and his desire to push his own unhappiness to an extreme, for it is only through extreme violence or in supreme gestures that the "poor" come a bit closer to "happiness." Gosta represents the "lost dog wandering about somewhere," preventing Thérèse's union with Florent. Her words will be echoed by Orpheus in *Eurydice*, who also knows and assumes the weight of responsibility for others. To his graceless father, also a poor café musician, Orpheus says: "I could not live, if I knew you were dying somewhere." [9]

III   Y avait un prisonnier *and* Le Voyageur sans bagage

Y avait un prisonnier (1935) and *Le Voyageur sans bagage* (written in 1936 and first produced in 1937) present two unpretentious heroes who seek merely to disappear from society. The "prisoner" of the earlier play is Ludovic, for whom time has stopped during a fifteen-year jail sentence. He has now been released, but upon seeing the transformation of his family, for whom time has been relentless, he is shocked and almost wishes he were still in prison. He had married "a flower," and now finds an unrecognizable woman who has had plastic surgery to restore her youthful appearance. "That's my wife? I dreamed of her as being young, young, magnificent, strong, stronger than I. With an animal-like arrogant good health to make up for my pallor and my skinny arms . . . with clear and pure laughter to compensate for my sadness. . . ." [10] His disillusionment is completed by hearing her relate the episodes in her life during his imprisonment.

Ludovic and La Brebis, a mute jail mate who has been freed together with the hero, are portraits of purity and simplicity: the first thing they seek upon leaving prison are the birds and the beasts, the pleasures offered by nature and not the luxury and hypocrisy offered by Ludovic's family. The two ex-convicts, in protest against all that they have witnessed, barricade themselves in the smoking room of the offshore yacht on which the action of the play takes place. The only person they will admit is Ludovic's best friend, Marcellin, whom they question about his life during the past fifteen years. His responses amount to zero, convincing Ludovic that he must escape this milieu; Marcellin, whom he so closely resembled in every way and who is symbolic of his attachment to reality, has changed both physically and spiritually. Ludovic, no longer having anything in common with Marcellin, must retreat into the realm of his own illusions.

Ludovic's friends and the family physician decide that he should be confined to "a villa in southern France" (an asylum) where he will find psychiatric help, ostensibly because he is unwilling to adjust to society by going into business and working, but actually because they would like to "get rid of him," fearing that he has learned too much about his relatives' dishonesty in their business accounts. Ludovic, however, knows that the asylum has no exit, and he and La Brebis, in a desperate attempt at freedom, jump overboard and begin swimming, taking the one chance in ten that they will reach the distant shore.

Ludovic's decision, like that of the heroes discussed in the preceding pages, is to make no compromise with society. His unaffected purity will survive only in the company of the tongueless La Brebis, who symbolizes a society free of corruption and injustice, but since *Y avait un prisonnier* is a *pièce noire*, the near-insane act of attempting to swim to shore must be interpreted as unsuccessful and resulting in the death of the ever unyielding hero.

Le Voyageur sans bagage is analogous in plot and characters to *Y avait un prisonnier*. Gaston is a soldier interned in an asylum because he has suffered amnesia. Although he is perfectly happy because he has no "past baggage" to carry, society presently interrupts his happiness, for a man with no past is frightening. Gaston is forced into his supposed family by a philanthropic Duchess who maintains that "our past is the best part of us," and by a lawyer who sees in Gaston a fortune in the form of a government pension to the family of a mutilated soldier. Stiff and stodgy Madame Renaud accepts him simply because a mother could scarcely do otherwise, as does Gaston's supposed sister-in-law, Valentine, whose husband is aware that his wife had been seduced by his brother (Gaston).

As the play progresses, we learn that the "real" son, Jacques Renaud, used to behave most despicably toward the domestic help. Upon hearing this the heretofore indifferent Gaston begins to experience troubled emotions. When he hears of Jacques Renaud's malicious fight with his schoolmate, his sentiments toward the Renaud family become violently hateful. The past that this supposed family has recreated for him is so repulsive that Gaston refuses it and all of its characters. His refusal is treated as madness; he is told that no one can reject his past, that he must either "belong" or return to the asylum.

The denouement of the play is provided by a melodramatic "recognition scene" which, avoiding entirely the moral issue of assuming responsibility for one's past actions, dramatizes the decision of the hero: a little English boy, to whom Gaston has confided the secret of an identifying scar (a scar known, however, to Valentine) on his body, is permitted to "claim" the amnesia victim as his nephew. Valentine, unless she wishes to reveal her adultery, must remain silent. Thus, Gaston brings about the symbolic death of Jacques Renaud, frees himself from the malignant clutches of a society that refuses to tolerate a man without a past, and escapes, in body if not in spirit, from the particularly abhorrent past being forced upon him.

Le Voyageur sans bagage would obviously be, were its ending and beginning reversed, Jean Anouilh's happiest comedy, for an escape into amnesia provides the perfect vehicle for the rejection of a former self and the creation of a pure illusion. As it stands, however, it is a *pièce noire*. The past is inescapable, whether it recalls painful experiences as it does for Gaston (and Thérèse in *La Sauvage*, and Marc in *Jézabel*), or the nostalgic longing for childhood which, while representing purity, innocence, beauty, and passion (as for Ludovic in *Y avait un prisonnier*), leads inevitably to disaster.

Through Gaston, Anouilh expresses his horror and contempt for the post-World War I bourgeoisie.[11] As Harold Clurman has observed: "In *Traveler Without Luggage*, anathemizing his past, Anouilh became a typical voice of a whole generation in a similar state of revulsion." [12] Although he cannot remember his past, Gaston assumes that, since he was found in a trainload of prisoners returning from Germany, he must have been at the front during the Great War. He only hopes that he has not killed anyone during the war, and part of his fear of recalling the past is due to the fact that he may have hurled "hard things against the poor flesh of man that a rose thorn causes to bleed." The impervious Duchess, who knows nothing of the realities of war, answers: "What kind of nonsense is that? I choose to believe, rather, that you were a hero," to which Gaston replies: "A hero is a pretty vague concept

in times of war. Slanderers, misers, the envious, and the cowardly
are all condemned to be heroes side by side and in about the same
way," [13] demonstrating with Pascalian eloquence the relativity of
heroism and the fact that man's virtue does not lie in his ability to
kill.

This scene is counterbalanced by the fifth tableau of the play, in
which Gaston, in his room at the Renauds' home, awakens to a
menagerie of stuffed birds and animals which he had supposedly
killed in his youth. The effect is traumatic. He is revolted by the
sight of birds that had been trapped in bird lime and then finished
off with a knife, and beasts that had been killed with a slingshot;
he is horrified by the thought that he could have done other than
caress the weasels, throw nuts to the squirrels, and feed the birds
with bread crumbs from his hand. His compassion is as boundless
as his sense of guilt for the sins of Jacques Renaud. Gaston is the
pacifist of his time, preaching love, not war.

In the second and fourth tableaus, other cruelties ascribed to
Jacques are revealed by the Renaud family; the scene is witnessed
by the servants through a round window, creating a play-within-a-
play effect that intensifies the unreality of Gaston's identity. We
learn that Jacques had broken a dog's paw with a stone, played
with knives and rifles, and crippled a friend by pushing him down
a flight of stairs. He was also a swindler and the seducer of his
brother's wife, Valentine, who, in a fit of jealousy, had stabbed
him with her hairpin, inflicting the identifying scar on his body.
He detested his mother and lived in her home for one year without speaking to her; when he left for the war, he refused to go to
her room to be kissed good-bye, maintaining that it was she who
should make the first step toward reconciliation. It is not surpris-
ing that Madame Renaud is accused by the uncomprehending
Duchess of not behaving maternally enough, not rolling at Gaston's feet in adoration, when her "son" is restored to her.

Another great source of chagrin to Gaston is that the person he
is supposed to be had no close friend. He muses: "I think there is
nothing more consoling to a man than a reflection of his childhood
in the eyes of a former little friend. It's a pity. I had even hoped, I
must admit, to get my memory back through this imaginary
friend." [14] Friendship, it will be recalled, was an important element so lacking in Anouilh's childhood, and since it comes closer
to the author's ideal, we see Gaston asking first about his friend,

and then about any young woman he may have loved. The hero continues: "Among the thousands of possible memories, it is precisely the memory of a friend that I called to mind with the most tenderness. I built everything on the memory of that imaginary friend. Our marvelous walks, the books we discovered together, a girl we both loved and that I sacrificed to him and even . . . my saving his life one day when our boat capsized. But, if I am your son, I will have to get accustomed to a truth very different from my dream." [15]

By the time Gaston has completed the investigations of his past, he is able to define himself as a being filled with hatred, wounds, and remorse, a being untouched by joy or enthusiasm. His decision to run away, to reject his past and the family that claims him, is prevented by Valentine, who knows that Gaston is, indeed, Jacques Renaud. It is she who attempts to impose a sense of universal and existential responsibility upon the man who has lived life—regardless of whether or not he remembers what his life has been—until death removes that responsibility: "You know it is not only I who am closing in on you and want to keep you. It's all women, all men . . . even the well-disposed dead who sense vaguely that you are trying to leave them abruptly. . . . You can't escape so many people, Jacques. And whether you like it or not, you'll have to belong to someone or else go back to the asylum." Gaston refuses to listen and dismisses Valentine, who represents reality, as though she were unreal: "Get out now. . . . You have played your role." [16]

Gaston's parting message to the Renauds, and the conclusion of the play, is that Jacques Renaud lies dead in some German grave, that his family should no longer fear to love him or see anything ugly in his memory, and that he, Gaston, the amnesia victim, exists *as Gaston,* despite all of their contrivances. Gaston seeks happiness, as does Marc in *Jézabel,* by escaping the past and becoming "an orphan without memories."

IV Roméo et Jeannette

The heroine of *Roméo et Jeannette* (1945) is similar to the central character in Saul Bellow's *The Last Analysis*: she is determined to undergo a baptism of filth and squalor in order to recover her true self. By shamelessly exposing her immorality to her Romeo, she believes that she will find the path of self-renewal.

Jeannette's sister Julia is engaged to Frédéric. One day the couple, together with Frédéric's polished and respectable mother, pay a visit to Julia's slovenly family, which consists of a drunken father and a sister and brother (Jeannette and Lucien), all of whom have a large assortment of bewildering idiosyncrasies. Frédéric, upon seeing Jeannette, falls almost instantly in love with her. She returns his love, and although her feelings are "pure" within her own soul, to the eyes of others her love is tainted with the sordidness of her past life and the unrelenting insistence of one of her distasteful yet wealthy lovers. Frédéric realizes that he cannot marry the savage Jeannette who, unlike her sister Julia, has been unable to overcome the effects of a highly objectionable family and a vile milieu. He becomes increasingly aware that he must leave her when Julia, in her jealousy, attempts suicide by poison.

In her rejection, Jeannette angrily accepts the marriage proposal of her wealthy lover, and during the course of the celebration at his mansion she slips away in order to show her white gown to Frédéric. Once she finds him, she proposes that the two drown themselves together, so that they will not have to live out the ugliness of their respective marriages. Frédéric refuses, however, arguing (in a scene reminiscent of *Antigone*) that death is just as absurd as the grotesque adventure of a life that must be lived. He then leaves with Julia. Jeannette begins walking out to the sea, so far out that the tide will have risen before she can return to safety. Frédéric spots her, in her symbolic white dress, goes out to join her, and the two drown together.

Jeannette's fruitless struggle to free herself from evil and the subsequent solution by suicide is similar to the theme of *La Sauvage*. Jeannette's family, like Thérèse's, has reached the heights of grotesqueness and disunity. When Julia brings her fiancé and her future mother-in-law home for the momentous asking of her hand in marriage, there is no one to receive them; the house is filthy and in complete disarray, with not a bit of food awaiting the hungry travelers. Julia knows that her father is out drinking and gambling, that her sister is at some tryst in the woods or on the deserted beach, and that her brother Lucien, who was once a bright student anxious to earn a living and who is now a torpid cynic separated from his wife, is locked in his room where he spends the entire day reading.

Julia describes at length to her fiancé the way her sister dresses in dirty rags and torn curtains, unmindful that parts of her flesh may be showing through her dresses and stockings. (The wedding gown that Jeannette dons at the end of the play is symbolic of a new identity that replaces the rags of her sordid past.) She contrasts her own orderliness, cleanliness, diligence, and honesty with Jeannette's disorder, slovenliness, laziness, and deceptions. Frédéric, however, is like Florent in *La Sauvage*: he is good, kind, pure, limpid, and honest. Everything in the bizarre household makes him laugh, and he excuses all without taking offense. He is no longer attracted to the neat and orderly Julia, but to the savage Jeannette. He is intrigued by her "gang," the Aces of Spades, who tattoo their bodies with penknife gashes and chew red paper, baptized "*mininistatfia*," which gives them strength. He desires her suntanned body, dirty though it may be.

After Frédéric's mother has killed a rooster found in the back yard so that the travelers may have something to eat, Jeannette protests violently the slaughter of her "Léon." Frédéric tries gently to explain the realities of life to her, reasoning that the blame for the injustices in life lies nowhere: "*c'est la vie.*" It is not his fault that he is his mother's son, nor is it her fault that she eats the meat only of animals she does not know. These arguments afford little consolation to Jeannette, who accepts neither compromise nor concession: "When I am old and understand everything, as others do, I know that I too will say that nothing is anybody's fault. It must be good, all of a sudden, to accept everything, to excuse everything, and never again revolt against anything." [17] She refuses to grow up, and the perpetuation of her childhood in her adult life is what leads her, as it does so many of Anouilh's heroines, to inevitable disaster.

As soon as Jeannette realizes that Frédéric is in love with her and not her sister Julia, she begins to smear herself by examining in his presence the slime in which she has been wallowing since the age of fifteen; she clamors for recognition of her ugliness in contrast with Julia's beauty and purity. Frédéric is nevertheless determined to have Jeannette for his wife, and in a hideout in the woods the wonder of their love is poignantly captured. They hardly know each other, yet feel bound to each other in a way that is beyond Frédéric's comprehension: "I do not know you, and yet this very evening you are going to be my wife. My wife and a little brother, both at the same time, for life and for death—this little stranger with her serious face. How simple it all is." [18]

Jeannette is Anouilh's concept of the stranger in society. She is rigid in her refusal to compromise, has a strong sense of honor and duty, and is a savage in revolt against superficial concepts of devotion. For Jeannette, engagement and marriage, the ceremony with white flowers in a church and the vows, bear military obligations: "If I ever say to a boy: from now on I am your wife, and we share good and evil between us, it would be as a soldier with his captain, and I'd rather my arms be cut off [than go back on my word]." [19]

Instead of facing those challenges of adulthood, Jeannette would prefer to remain always a child, to play, gang against gang, and "capture" Julia, of whom she is jealous, tie her to a tree and scalp her. She regrets that adults cannot fight in this way, that Frédéric cannot take his knife and cut open her heart to see how clean and red it is inside, even though she is dirty outside.

Jeannette's brother, Lucien, represents the boy who has grown up and donned the attire of adulthood. He is bitter and cynical because he is a cuckold; he is rude and uncouth, and seeks the destruction of others' happiness. He predicts that Frédéric, married to Julia, will make an excellent and happy cuckold, whereas he, Lucien, is a sad one. He advises Frédéric to marry Julia, have children, be a man with a profession and money, and make all the compromises that life demands, for that is the only way God will leave him alone and not torment him. By doing something "good," such as running off with Jeannette, he is bound to lose, according to Lucien, for God would not like the idea. Lucien's God, as described above in Chapter 2, is the God that dislikes lovers. At present Lucien is awaiting an assignment in the Ivory Coast so that he can live far away from white society's ideas of love and try to find his true self, for when asked by his sister where the other members of the family are, he answers: "I never know where the others are. I hardly know where I am myself, around here." [20]

At the very end of the play, as Jeannette and Frédéric die together, Lucien receives the long-awaited African assignment from the hands of the postman who used to call out *"Les enfants!"* each time he delivered the mail. Lucien now responds to the postman that "there are no more children," signifying that the concepts of purity and innocence known to Jeannette, to Frédéric, and to himself are now all dead.

V   La Grotte *and* L'Orchestre

La Grotte (1961) and *L'Orchestre* (1962), two of Anouilh's more recent plays, are clearly *pièces noires*. The point of departure of the first is a *fait accompli*: the apparent murder of the cook by a jealous lover. An investigation of the real cause of death ensues, in a flashback directed by the Author, who is a character in the play. It takes place on the two levels of the stage décors: upstairs, an immense, palatial salon; downstairs, the kitchen—a dark cave (*"la grotte"*).

The police chief's questioning of all the residents of the household is a classic illustration of "justice": the Count, who had found the cook's body, is exempt from any prodding, while the valet and the coachman are subjected to extensive interrogation. During the course of the questioning we learn that the Count was the cook's lover twenty-five years previously, when she was "ravishing"; he unknowingly fathered an illegitimate son (the Young Seminarist in the play). The cook's most recent lover had been the debauched coachman, Léon Lacasse, who had a good alibi when the crime was committed: he had been drinking all evening with the owner of the Three Pipes Café. The only persons who had been in the kitchen immediately prior to the cook's stabbing were, according to the police version of the story, the Count and the Seminarist; the latter has been in the unsuspecting Count's hire as Latin tutor for his children. It is only on the day of the assassination that the Count discovers the identity of his son.

Adèle, the downtrodden kitchen maid who loves the Seminarist from afar, has been made pregnant by Léon. She is martyrized by all: by the cook who discovered that her son was in love with Adèle, by the Seminarist who insists that she be pure, by the despicable valet who tries to "sell" her to a café owner in Oran, and, finally, by the Author who shouts at her that her mentality is all wrong.

The cook has throughout the play refused to allow her son to marry Adèle. Although he would be willing to be a father to the baby that Adèle is trying desperately and with much physical pain to abort, the cook tells her son that rather than have him marry a kitchen maid she would prefer to strangle Adèle to death and then spend the rest of her life washing dishes in prison, which is no different from washing them in *"la grotte."* She tells him that she has made him a Seminarist so that he might avoid marrying a peasant, and to impress upon the highly sensitive young man what a peasant is, she kills a rabbit before his eyes.

The Seminarist finally decides to ask the Countess to help Adèle, whom he describes as "a being who still remains pure and innocent in the filth in which she wallows." [21] The Countess decides to do something "nice" for Adèle: she herself will go down to the kitchen with her youngest son and ask Adèle to be his godmother. She will cause the race of the rich and the race of the poor to mingle harmoniously. Up to this point in the play Adèle had presented the image of a timid creature who submitted whenever anyone raised his voice to her, a pathetic peasant girl without Joan of Arc's mettle; but in the scene in which she refuses the Countess' offer she shows herself to be a true Anouilh savage heroine. She expresses her contempt for both the downstairs and the upstairs worlds: for her father, who made her a victim of his drunken desires; for Léon, who seduced her in the filth of the stable; for the cook, who prepares her brews to induce abortion and serves them with blows; for the Count and the Countess; for the nuns, who used to punish her in winter by having her sit outdoors on a pail of cold water and forcing her to ask God's pardon; for the Seminarist, whom she loves; for God, whom she does not love.

Adèle's virulent reaction causes the upstairs and the downstairs abruptly to separate once again. Tension mounts in the kitchen; accusations are flung in all directions, knives are seized, the lights go out. When the kitchen is again lighted, the cook is lying half-dead on the kitchen table; she is nursing her own wounds, on the one hand protesting that she is as strong as her father who had his leg amputated without anesthesia during the Crimean War, on the other, recalling the beauty and the happiness of her youth, when the Count loved her.

The play ends with the police chief's triumphant announcement of his apprehension of the killer—Léon—by a forced confession. The Author banishes the police chief from the stage to his realm of "nothingness," implying that the reality of the situation lies in the illusion that the Author has been trying to create and not in the "evidence" presented by the police. The Author turns to the audience with apologies if he has failed, and the curtain falls.

The central theme of *La Grotte* is, of course, that an insurmountable barrier exists between the world of the aristocracy and the world of the kitchen, and that it is on the "downstairs" world that we must focus to see the microcosm of the sordid realities of life (a thought similar to that of Arnold Wesker in *The Kitchen*). Anouilh, as has been pointed out, purposely divides the stage horizontally, and demonstrates that when the world is clearly divided in two the kitchen inhabitants, even though they may be ill-nourished, ill-treated and ill-paid, are nevertheless relatively calm and tranquil. It is only when the upstairs attempts, under the humanizing influence of the Countess, to penetrate into the darkness of the kitchen that disaster is wrought. (This is an expression of Anouilh's conservatism and his aversion for leftist tendencies to improve the lot of the poor. He demonstrates his preference for the "old days," when there was a clear separation of the races, when servants, by accepting their inescapable fate, were afforded a certain peace of mind and were not subjected to the humiliation caused by the condescending attitude of the rich.)

Anouilh envisages an ordered world in *"la grotte,"* where a sense of honor and duty prevails among the domestic employees. The cook's "code of honor" prevents her from revealing the name of her attacker; the butler's dignity lies in keeping his place and respecting the different traditions of the aristocracy without trying to comprehend them; the kitchen maid's sense of justice bids her to nurse the little kitchen helper tenderly when he is sick, but to beat him when he is well, because "when you get big, you'll beat someone smaller than you. That's justice. And neither you nor I can change it" [22]; and the much abused kitchen helper's sense of honor demands that his potato peeling be performed to perfection even though his reward may be in the form of blows, and forbids him from speaking ill of others, even under police questioning.

Each of these characters represents a virtue of Anouilh's heroic race. Marie-Jeanne, the cook, is the personification of courage in the face of deception, abuse, scorn, and death. She has devastating vision, bordering on cruelty, in her prophecies of Adèle's future life—eternal scrubbing of floors, suffering without pleasure under brutal lovers—combined with warnings never to become involved with anyone "upstairs," the punishment for which is black (not blue) blood in the heart which can never be spat up.

Marie-Jeanne knows the torment of this, for she has been the Count's mistress and, ever since, black blood has been flowing in her veins. The bloodletting that Marie-Jeanne practices is common to kitchen inmates: scorn in the form of serving to the "rich" the worst foods, leftovers, and reheated coffee, and drunken celebration when anyone "upstairs" dies. In spite of her coarseness, however, the Author gives Marie-Jeanne great delicacy by explaining that he was inspired to write this play by a Rimbaud poem that he loves, written to someone named Jeanne-Marie. By writing the play for the cook, he hopes to bring her into the realm of Rimbaud's "possible ideas" and to give her "two *sous* of reality."

Adèle represents the innocence and purity of "*la sauvage*" in the midst of corruption and debasement. She accepts the bitter brews prepared by Marie-Jeanne to help her abort, but she tenaciously refuses to reveal Léon's guilt. Adèle is a universal, protecting mother, self-sacrificing and self-negating. The Author in the play says: "It is for her, too—to render homage that she never would have received in her misery—that I wanted to write this play, and I wanted it to be a beautiful play." [23]

The naïve and sedulous kitchen helper, who cannot believe that mental labor is harder than physical labor since "nobody sweats from the head," is the faithful and humble perfectionist. He perseveres in his duty, which is to peel potatoes beautifully, and builds more stately mansions for his soul: he will work hard, someday be the owner of a restaurant, economize, forget all about the blows he has received, become a man, free and rich—and even a king, if he will. He almost assumes the dimensions of a Redeemer: "He is the Grotto's hope; the one who will cause it to disintegrate. . . . Yes, you will have your glimmer of hope at the end, rest assured. By his courage and his innocence, the little boy, the humblest and the most helpless, will succeed, in spite of all, in destroying the Grotto." [24]

The butler has the sound political sense that Anouilh admires; he upholds the established social order that separates the rich and the poor. He would never think of joining the union, lest it upset the rules of the game and cause France to become "worm-riddled"; he bears the name "Romain," signifying his traditional rigor; he insists upon playing the role of the perfect, discreet, dignified butler, safeguard of the aristocracy. According to Romain, Louis XV had the sorry idea of having a fully prepared table in the Trianon come up automatically from the kitchens, so that there would be no butlers or servants when he wanted privacy with Madame du Barry. The theory that the elimination of butlers is the perdition of kings is demonstrated by Romain: King Louis, who had carved his own chicken, seventeen years later saw his grandson's head "carved" by the Revolutionaries. (It is at this point in the play that the police chief begins to suspect Romain of having killed the cook, perhaps because she had miscarved a roast.)

Somewhere between the kitchen and the "upstairs" hovers the Seminarist, whose father is the Count and whose mother is the cook. He fears the "upstairs," and at the same time is horrified by the lies employed by his mother to obtain him his position as Latin tutor to the Count's children, and by her taunting vulgarity in urging him to be unscrupulously mercenary. Being "neither from above nor from below," the Seminarist has hidden his true self under his black robe and has turned to God for refuge, but we know that, for Anouilh, God is asleep. The Seminarist finds that God is "cold and silent." In his bewilderment, it is Adèle's gentleness that provides the warmth he is seeking.

The clearly defined upstairs realm opposed to *"la grotte"* is inhabited by the Count, the Countess, and their children. The Count is Anouilh's third hero type: sometimes guided by conscience, yet never rising to the heights of heroism. Long ago, he had seduced the cook; now he is married to a sweet, gentle noblewoman twenty years younger than he. Although she would like him to be less serious, more youthful and passionate, the Count now chooses to play the role of the well-bred, affable, tolerant, and witty gentleman. Dispassion is his hallmark: "I shall never utter a cry. I leave that to the animals, and to furious, passionate men who are similar to animals. Man has the good fortune to possess an articulate language and certain standards, which permit him to express in a decent manner the nuances of his mind and, if he insists, of his heart. He doesn't have to utter a cry. . . ." [25]

The Count, like Anouilh, believes that each individual must play his role as decided by fate. Since destiny has placed him on the upper level of the house, he assumes no responsibility for the lower level and attempts to dissuade his wife from going "down-stairs" to invite Adèle to be their son's godmother: "The poor don't need your words and your good intentions. They don't need your charity. They thirst for one thing . . . to be respected." [26] He explains that the poor, since they are aware of the inordinate difference between themselves and the rich, demand that the rich impose upon themselves the duty of behaving correctly. He reveals to his wife that it was Marie-Jeanne who had proudly refused his offer of marriage, even though she loved him, because they were not of the same world. Having been forced to face this reality, the Count now considers it his duty to leave Marie-Jeanne alone in the kitchen, to allow her to cherish in peace the memory of her naïve sacrifice.

The Countess, however, has never previously associated with the "downstairs" world; in her illusions, she sees its inhabitants as much simpler and humbler. She is not convinced that her gesture will offend Adèle, and is shocked into reality only by Adèle's outburst of vehement scorn and hatred, while the Count stands by in an "I told you so" manner.

La Grotte has all of the markings of a typical *pièce noire*, but is a more remarkable play because of Anouilh's use of the very special Pirandellian dramatic technique so evocative of *Six Characters in Search of an Author*. In Chapter 8, *La Grotte* will be analyzed in that light.

L'Orchestre, a play with autobiographic overtones, is also a typical *pièce noire*, with the heroine's escape taking the form of suicide. The curtain rises on a bar in which an orchestra is rendering a gay piece of music. All of the performers are women, with the exception of Monsieur Léon, a droll, lanky pianist who is married to a cripple. As soon as the piece is finished, the women begin chattering about men, recipes, knitting, and furniture cleaning methods. During the course of these exchanges Madame Hortense, the double bass and orchestra leader, while maintaining reserve and graciousness toward the clients, utters deprecating remarks intended to underscore Léon's inferiority and his lack of virility. The members of the orchestra, who are supposed paragons of femininity, engage in a crescendo of insults that continue on into the next sweet piece of music, while they kick one another and otherwise give vent to their belligerence.

Suzanne Delcias, who is in love with the pianist, is jealous of Madame Hortense. As she is performing on the violoncello, Suzanne threatens to commit suicide. Léon's distress at her words is inversely supported by the music, which becomes increasingly gay and which is positively arousing when Suzanne decides that they should die together.

The particular piece of music that is being played ("Cocardes et Cocoricos") fills Madame Hortense with pride in her superior talent and with patriotism. She boasts of her refusal to play in Vichy during the Occupation, and suggests that Suzanne was a traitor because she played for the Nazis. Suzanne irritably defends herself by claiming that orchestra members were all of the Resistance, and that they took the risk of playing off key in the presence of German officers who were known to be good musicians. Léon attempts to calm the two by demonstrating the absurdity of judging musical talent on the basis of collaboration and resistance.

A conversation ensues between Pamela and Patricia, both of whom have aged, senile mothers. The daughters give nursing care to their mothers, but do so without affection or comprehension. They have been hardened by poverty, and are forced to impose upon their helpless mothers a discipline that will permit the daughters to continue their struggle for existence.

At this point Suzanne disappears from the stage, the orchestra begins to play a heavy, sensual Cuban melody, and the pianist groans some words to the effect that his mother is the only one who ever loved him. With the announcement that Suzanne has committed suicide in the ladies' room Léon loses his sanity, and the curtain falls to the strains of a gracious gavotte.

The message of this short play is clear: the orchestra is the "kitchen" of the outside world. The players are imprisoned in their poverty and insignificance, and the music they create serves only to obscure their oppression from the "other" world; their only means of escape from the sordidness that surrounds them are death and insanity. L'Orchestre, like the other "black" plays, provides no practical solution to human problems.

The typical conflict in the pièces noires may be described as the "pure" individual's search for self-fulfillment or for some ideal in a corrupt society that demands incessant compromises with his integrity. In the early plays, it is the hero's past experiences that prevent his integration into society (Gaston, Thérèse, Eurydice). Later it is clearly the "romantic" and intransigent nature of the individual that is responsible for the revolt (Antigone, Jeannette, Medea). In both cases, the characters have no recourse but to escape reality, either through solitude and isolation (*La Sauvage, Le Voyageur sans bagage, Y avait un prisonnier, Jézabel*) or through actual or symbolic death (*L'Hermine, Roméo et Jeannette, L'Orchestre, La Grotte*).

CHAPTER 4

Pièces roses

IF in the *pièces noires* society triumphs over the absolute ideal
and compels the heroes to seek a tragic form of escape, in the
pièces roses Anouilh's characters escape black reality through fantasy, illusion, and changing personality. It is as if the author felt
that the world, with its fiendish problems, lacked and needed the
sense of humor that he attempted to provide in "pink" situations.
No shortage of material faced Anouilh, for he was aware that ex-
aggeration is the essence of humor, and that the world is full of
pygmies spouting exaggerated nonsense.

I Le Bal des voleurs

Le Bal des voleurs (1932) despite a few dark moments is essen-
tially a "pink" fantasy. The plot revolves around the wealthy Lady
Hurf and her nieces, Juliette and Eva, as they come into contact
with three professional thieves. One of the thieves, Gustave, falls
in love with Juliette, who in turn falls in love with one of the
many diverse personalities of Gustave. Since he must incessantly
change his disguise to avoid detection by the police, Gustave is
unable to remember which of his personalities had attracted Juliette. He spends the entire play changing costumes, each time actually becoming the character he is impersonating. The masquerade is a diversion for the audience, as they cannot take Gustave's
struggles with his personality too seriously.

As for Lady Hurf, the most lucid of all, she goes along with the
comical masquerade and the other absurdities of the situation,
playing her role because she is bored. Whether inadvertently or
purposefully, she has erroneously read the announcements for a
flower ball (*"bal des fleurs"*) to be held in town one evening as a
thieves' ball (*"bal des voleurs"*). Gustave has the opportunity to
raid her mansion after his cohorts, disguised as Spanish nobles,
and Lady Hurf and her entourage, in their thieves' costumes, have

set out for the masked ball. Lady Hurf, her nieces and their es-
corts, the DuPont-DuForts, however, are turned away from the
ball because of their inappropriate costumes. (Juliette has meanwhile escaped her aunt's group in order to help Gustave steal the
valuables from Lady Hurf's home.) The DuPont-DuForts de-
nounce the thieves (who are in their Spanish noble costumes),
but when the police arrive on the scene the real thieves are over-
looked and the DuPont-DuForts, who look most like thieves in
their costumes, are arrested. *Schein ist sein.*

The fanciful nature of this play provides Anouilh with a vehicle
through which to demonstrate his concern with the relativity of
truth, for thieves can be honest men and honest men thieves,
bored women can be tricksters and clarinet players detectives, according to how they wish to appear and how others care to look at
them. The multiplicity of the human personality underlies the in-
stability of "truth": man is too complex, possesses too many con-
flicting personalities, ever to become a peaceful unity.

The series of masquerades in *Le Bal des voleurs* humorously
illustrates this point. One thief appears in his moustache and wig,
the second enters in the guise of a woman who rents chairs, and
the third is disguised as a young girl. The next scene brings the
three back in military disguise, until they notice that the wealthy
protagonist's pearls come from a ruined Spanish family. They exit
and reenter, one thief as a very noble—too noble—old Spaniard,
the second as a peer of Spain, and the third as an ecclesiastical
secretary. Later, two of the thieves are obliged to become handsome young men in order to appeal to the young heroines. The
last tableau of the play, in which everyone is dressed for the
thieves' ball (including even the seemingly innocent clarinet
player in the costume of a Scotland Yard detective), symbolizes
the facility with which we can "make ourselves over" according to
the particular circumstances in which we happen to be.

Although the play illustrates Charles Chaplin's dictum that the
basic element of comedy lies in doing mad things in a perfectly
solemn way,[1] a strain of solemnity without comic intent runs
through Gustave, Lady Hurf, and her older niece Eva. Gustave is
somewhat similar to Frantz in *L'Hermine* and to Gaston in *Le
Voyageur sans bagage*: he belongs to the "poor" race. He tries to
dissuade Juliette from running off with him, pleading that she
knows only happiness and luxury, and nothing about hiding from

the police and being afraid. Besides, having neither father nor mother, no "past" heritage, he will be prevented from obtaining Lady Hurf's consent to their marriage.

Society has marked Gustave as a thief without seeking to know why he has become one or why he continues to be one in view of the fact that stolen goods are difficult to resell and command a very small price on the "market." Nevertheless, Juliette's happiness at being in love with Gustave, her adroitness in stealing the most valuable art works from her aunt's drawing room, and the felicitous creation of an illusory, noble "father" for Gustave succeed in calming her lover's pecuniary fears and her aunt's genealogical qualms, as the play resumes its upward "pink" swing.

Lady Hurf, although playing out the comedy of errors with sparkling humor, inspires within us a fleeting pity, for she reveals that under her mask of gaiety lies a solitude which, intensified with the passage of time, clamors for bigger and better illusions to bury it. Lady Hurf describes herself as a bored old carcass who has had in life everything that a woman might reasonably or unreasonably desire: money, power, lovers. Now in her old age she feels as alone as when she was a child being punished in the corner, and in between her childhood and the present there has been a long stretch of stark, if noisy, solitude, worse than any other period of solitude. She confesses to her older niece Eva that her only recourse has been escape into the realm of illusion, such as she has created on the evening of the thieves' ball.

Eva too, is reminiscent of Anouilh's other symbolic figures of solitude. She has never known love; life's experiences are harsh for her even though she is surrounded by luxury. She envies the "purity" of Juliette, to whom she says with bitterness: "You have never, as I, made love without being in love. You have no pearls around your neck, no ring on your finger. I am sure you are completely naked under your white linen dress, and you are twenty years old, and you are in love." [2]

As Eva watches the happy couple wander into the garden, she turns in resignation to Lady Hurf with the words: "And off I go, to continue playing my role of a charming and highly successful young lady." Lady Hurf answers: "My poor Eva, what do you expect? Our story is over. . . . The comedy was a hit only for those who played it with all their youth, indeed, because they were acting out their youth, which is always a success. They didn't even notice the comedy." [3] Thus, even in Anouilh's most farcical of the *pièces roses*, poetic fantasy and illusion do not succeed completely in masking the author's immutable awareness of life's prosaic and tragic darkness.

II Le Rendez-vous de Senlis

The aura of fantasy enveloping *Le Bal des voleurs* is carried over to Anouilh's second *pièce rose, Le Rendez-vous de Senlis* (written in 1937 and first produced in 1941). This "pink" play is a strange mixture of drama, parody, comedy of manners and of character, a psychological portrait, a fantasy, a detective story with touches of vaudeville—in sum, as Anouilh laments, life itself.

Ashamed of the hypocrisy and avarice of his parents and of the hysteria and jealousy of his wife, Georges attempts to "shed his past" and escape into the arms of Isabelle, a naïve young girl who symbolizes detachment, purity, and love. He creates a set of ideal parents, hiring two actors to portray them. His intention is to introduce them, at a rendezvous in Senlis, to Isabelle, who is already familiar with them through conversations with Georges. His friend Robert (who is actually his wife's lover) will remain invisible, even though his place will be set at the table.

Because of an unsuccessful attempt by Georges' wife to shoot him, things at Senlis do not go off as planned. Isabelle is made aware of Georges' deception, but she forces the idealization to overrule reality and refuses to recognize Georges' sordid family life; she accepts happily the family, the friend, and the Georges that have been created by illusion. Being a *pièce rose, Le Rendez-vous de Senlis* permits Georges to accept Isabelle's somewhat frightening prospect of pure happiness; leaving his past forever behind him, he departs with her for the Pyrenees, where he will become an apiculturist.

Like Frantz in *L'Hermine* and Marc in *Jézabel*, Georges wants to create an ideal situation for the girl he loves. He conceives of the perfect father as a charming old man who nevertheless retains some perennial vestiges of youth, who knows how to be an older brother and a "pal," who is strong and reassuring and who inspires his son's confidence—in short, the father image that was lacking in Anouilh's own life. Moreover, the ideal father is highly consider-

ate of the domestic help, comprehending of the problems of even
the dishonest ones, and, above all, he is not "money-mad," contrary to the antipathetic fathers in many of Anouilh's plays.

Georges' ideal mother would be constantly worried about her
son, would, like a young girl in love, tremble and lose the thread
of conversation whenever he entered the room, would never have
any shopping to do, and would never leave him to pay social
visits. Once again we are presented with the mother image that
the young Anouilh could never enjoy because of his mother's constant drudgery to scrape together a living. Georges begs the actor
and actress hired to play the roles of his parents to bring to life the
lies that have stirred his beloved Isabelle's imagination; his very
life depends upon it.

As for his ideal friend, Robert, Georges has created in Isabelle's
mind a concept very similar to that in the mind of Gaston, the
amnesia victim in *Le Voyageur sans bagage*, who searches the
past for the friend whom he loved dearly and for whom he would
have sacrificed all.[4] Georges has a place set for the imaginary
Robert at Senlis, but arranges for him not to appear in the form of
an actor because he believes that no one can play the role of such
an idealized being.

The setting for the rendezvous in Senlis is also fanciful and illusory: Georges has rented a decrepit old house for a few days.
"With a little imagination," he tells the owner, "you can very easily live your entire lifetime in one evening."[5] The house contains
glued-together pieces of chairs and porcelain, wireless telephones,
and an ensemble of old souvenirs—a true "fading mansion"
evoked with nostalgia by Anouilh as a remembrance of good
things past.

The proprietor, as old and decrepit as the house, claims that
cares are eating her old body alive, to which Georges, with un-
feigned sadness, replies that cares seem to like young flesh, too.
She says plaintively that she would have liked to rent the home
for a whole year, not just a short period of time, to which Georges
retorts, in a symbolic image of the lease on happiness: "I, too,
Madame, would have liked to rent for the entire year. We all
would like to rent by the year but we never can rent for more than
a week or a day. Such is the image of life."[6] Later in the play
Anouilh's philosophy of the brevity of happiness is again expressed in similar terms of time: "How demanding we are. . . .

We start out by wanting not less than a lifetime of happiness, then we discover that we are fortunate to get a few stolen years. . . . After that, we are satisfied with one evening. . . . And then, suddenly, we are left with only five minutes, and we finally discover that five minutes are an infinite oasis of happiness." [7]

If the rendezvous in Senlis represents the triumph of illusion and spiritual idealization, Georges' household in Paris epitomizes the sordidness of reality and material decadence. His wealthy wife Henriette supports Georges' parents as well as his friend Robert and his wife Barbara (who is Georges' mistress). All have made the compromises that Thérèse Tarde's father in *La Sauvage* would have made had his savage daughter not rejected her wealthy suitor. Georges is not heroic: he did not refuse to marry Henriette, even though it was a marriage of convenience and without love. Now, his horror of their degenerate milieu forces him to seek escape in Isabelle's notion of his ideal family. When, at the end of the play, Georges decides to leave with Isabelle, he swears lasting hatred and disgust for his former mistress, while at the same time seeking absolution from her for his past sin of having wallowed with her in filth.

Barbara's husband Robert, Georges' supposed "friend," is very similar to the cynical Lucien in *Roméo et Jeannette;* he has donned a mask of resentment, iniquity, abomination, and cynicism. Although they were friends in poverty he now resents Georges' wealth, admitting nevertheless that he would have enjoyed a similar matrimonial opportunity. His bitterness is deepened by the fact that the *nouveau riche* Georges has hired him as a secretary and pays him a salary of three thousand francs per month, and he is ferociously happy that Henriette may divorce Georges, so that his "boss" will recall the taste of living from hand to mouth, traveling in the subway that smells of cold grease, and be submissive to a superior.

Now that Georges has become rich, Robert reveals to his wife his childhood envy of his friend's good looks and better grades in school. In his resentment, he blurts out his subconscious desire for the destruction of all Georges: "The beauty of revolutions is seeing people who had been happy die." [8] (His words will be echoed in a later play, *Pauvre Bitos,* by a pseudo-Robespierre.)

Robert is especially graphic in describing the unadulterated, repulsive sordidness of the *ménage à trois* formed by himself, his

wife, and Georges. The more Georges attempts to be gracious and
gentle, the more disgusting it pleases Robert to become. Having
learned that Georges has created in Isabelle's mind an image of
him as a perfect friend, Robert, the male "sauvage," becomes almost insane. It is hard to distinguish whether, in his ravings, he is
laughing or crying at the comedy that has been prepared for Isabelle, as it is hard to believe that his cruel mockery of Isabelle's
incredulity is genuine, for in his heart he envies Georges' ability to
escape reality. Because Robert has now been caught up in the
game, no one can stop his ravings. He will not be silenced. He will
(again, similar to the *Six Characters in Search of an Author*) play
out his role to the end, snatching off the masks of all the other
characters, and then he, too, will escape into the world of naked
images.

Captured by the spirit of Isabelle's fantasy, Georges and Robert
seize the straw that will permit them to savor the pleasures of
living in a world of pure illusion, making *Le Rendez-vous de
Senlis* a typical *pièce rose*.

III   Léocadia

Another of Anouilh's purely poetic fantasies is *Léocadia* (written in 1939 and first produced in 1940). A bored young prince,
Albert Troubiscoï, is left distraught when his precious Léocadia
accidentally strangles herself in a purely dramatic gesture. The
Duchess, the prince's aunt, tries to maintain for her nephew the
memory of his beloved by keeping their somewhat terrifying château and park exactly as they were when Léocadia was alive. To
play the role of the deceased she hires Amanda, a young milliner
who can pass for Léocadia's double. Amanda struggles against the
imposed mask and rebels against a counterfeit personality until
her true self triumphs over Léocadia's ghost. The prince reveals
that his inconsolable dream is feigned, and suggests that it is those
who surround him who are, perhaps, mad and cause him to seek
escape. Amanda and the prince, having now assumed their true
identities, finally succeed in communicating with each other in the
language of love.

Anouilh's two "races" are clearly represented in *Léocadia*, but,
since this is a "pink" play, a happy marriage between the two can
be achieved by allowing fantasy and illusion to transcend all frontiers. Amanda represents the "poor" race. Her hands are calloused

and her eyes are bloodshot from long hours of work in a millinery factory. The luxury and the unreality of the Pont-au-Bronc grounds fill her with wonder. Her encounter with the ice cream vendor, who is invited to jab her with a pin so that she can know whether she is awake or dreaming, is sheer comedy, yet Amanda does ask for her pin back, suggesting that the poor must protect their meager possessions.

The other persons in the Duchess' employ—the taxicab driver, the butler, the musicians, etc.—have been obliged to play their roles since the day two years earlier when Léocadia died and the clock of life stopped at Pont-au-Bronc. They have nothing to occupy them all day long; their only function is to await the prince's daily visit to the café that he haunted when Léocadia was alive. Such excessive idleness forces these poor workers into thinking themselves into Pascalian solitude.

The "rich" race is personified by the Duchess and her nephew, Prince Albert. The Duchess is a fairyland character, but even more fabulous than her personality is her wealth: her funds are inexhaustible; she owns dozens of famous masterpieces, has had an entire village reconstructed on her property at her own expense, and is making a good income from the religious items being sold in the basilica that is part of the reconstructed village. The Duchess is not only unbelievably wealthy but also immensely influential. Although she is gratified that her nephew and Léocadia did not visit any national monuments or fortifications during their love affair, since it might have been a bit difficult to have those constructions demolished and then rebuilt at Pont-au-Bronc, she is nevertheless confident that the "administration" would have given her the necessary permission. Since the Freemasons in the area have cut off the trains that brought worshipers to the Duchess' basilica, she has arranged with the Citroën automobile company to provide transportation for her income producers.

A descendant of the medieval French King Louis le Gros, the Duchess is concerned that now, seven hundred years after the reign of Louis, her nephew is dishonoring the names of Troubiscoï and d'Andinet d'Andaine by associating with taxidrivers and ice cream vendors, and by spending his evenings in a miserable little café, simply to keep alive the memory of Léocadia.

The prince is a phlegmatic dreamer, who also has calloused hands; not from an honest day's work, however, but from golf clubs and tennis racquets. His week is composed of seven Sundays. Cruel in his attitude toward Amanda, he mocks her poverty, her banality and the code of honor of her "race," which forbids her to accept a penny more than her due salary. The miracle is that Amanda can love such an inhuman prince, with his monocle and his mania, but that, of course, is Amanda's magic: she can render the repulsive attractive, the complicated simple, the unreal real, and the hypocritical sincere, just by being her honest and modest self.

When the butler brings Amanda the fur cape she has been obliged to don in playing the role of Léocadia she refuses it with the words: "Take it back to the château! *I* don't wear fur in the summertime. In summer, *I* feel warm." [9] Instead of ordering champagne as she was instructed to do in memory of Léocadia's preferences, Amanda requests anisette Marie Brizard with water: "I'd like to be *me* a moment, just to rest. And *I* am thirsty. And *I* don't like champagne." [10]

Amanda's words cause the entire Pont-au-Bronc setting to go out of focus: the music sounds off key, and the players seem unable to fulfill their roles. When Amanda utters the simple words "je vous aime," words which Léocadia could never have spoken because her speech was so complicated, Pont-au-Bronc goes completely topsy-turvy: the musicians play the wrong piece of music, the impeccable butler causes the champagne to spill over when he uncorks the bottle—the spell is broken. Amanda may now speak the truth: Léocadia did not love Albert, nor did he really love her.

The prince finally breaks down and, in an eloquent self-analysis, confesses to his ridiculousness. The scene is a marvelously objective revolt against the two concepts of rich and poor. He ascribes his foolishness to the fact that in his youth he had been raised by old women and old priests, and in adulthood he has led an extremely sheltered life, far out of contact with what Amanda calls "life." He valiantly defends himself against a society that is just as harsh to him as it is to the poor. The drunken proletariat is maligned for leading the country to destruction, paralyzing production, and reducing the birth rate, but the prince, too, is maligned for living in a sixteenth-century monument and bearing twenty-two insignificant titular names. The meanest peasant of France has no harder a time than the prince proving that he is not an imbecile, and the former, if he succeeds, is offered scholarships and encouraged to become President of the Republic, whereas a prince would be allowed no such incentives. For these reasons, the prince was drawn to Léocadia; comic and bizarre though she was, eating orchids and sleeping from daybreak to sunset only, she alone could provide him with a realization of what is "different" in life. She had unusual intelligence, great originality of thought and expression, and would never allow her flesh to be touched. These, for the prince, were the bitter joys of his love, and he is convinced that Amanda's foolish and banal concept of happiness could never replace what he felt for Léocadia.

Proud of his long tirade, the prince studies Amanda's reaction, which is one of hostile defiance. She then escapes into the garden to weep. As the sun's rays begin to shine on her, however, Amanda finds a certain ease in nature which the prince resents and which Léocadia had never possessed. If Léocadia went to bed at daybreak and ate orchids, Amanda now demonstrates to the prince the beauty and happiness of waking to the morning sun with a healthy appetite. She begins to devour large quantities of bread and butter, with coffee and milk, and shows no sign of sorrow or shame.

The vision somewhat frightens the prince, and as he wonders who this girl is, Amanda forces him to hold her. Prince Albert Troubiscoï finds the gesture of taking the milliner Amanda into his arms simple, true, easy, and sure. The Duchess, passing by and spotting the couple, takes aim and shoots a strange bird symbolic of Léocadia. The bird is buried in the Pont-au-Bronc park, and a new love lives.

Much of Anouilh's art in *Léocadia* lies in the fact that he is able to employ fantasy and illusion to allude to the most modern and realistic of man's problems. No practical solutions are offered, any more than they were in the *pièces noires,* but in the "pink" plays we are invited at least to stop playing hide-and-seek with ourselves and to relax without restraint in the enjoyment of natural sentiments that will always triumph over any artificially preserved sordid memories and illegitimate, illogical relationships. The happy plays of Anouilh seem almost unplanned and haphazard in their spontaneity, yet they are deliberate expressions of the rare moments of *"la vie en rose"* as seen by this predominantly tragic author.

CHAPTER 5

Pièces brillantes

THE overall levity of the "pink" plays is maintained through the first two *pièces brillantes, L'Invitation au Château,* (1947) and *Cécile, ou l'Ecole des pères* (1949), but is counterbalanced by the weight of ugly reality in the second two, *La Répétition, ou l'Amour puni* (1950) and *Colombe* (1951).

I   L'Invitation au Château

In *L'Invitation au Château,* a pleasantly jumbled fairy tale, Anouilh guides his puppet-like characters through a complex intrigue of errors. Frédéric, naïve and innocent, has fallen in love with the wealthy, acrimonious but beautiful Diana, who loves and has been rejected by Horace, Frédéric's far-from-innocent twin brother. To protect Frédéric from his blind love for Diana and to antagonize Diana, whom he really loves, Horace brings to the château the poor, insignificant dancer Isabelle to play the role of a dazzling young socialite. After an evening of imbroglio and mistaken identity, Frédéric and Isabelle, and Horace and Diana are united in the typical happy ending of Anouilh's lighter pieces.

L'Invitation au Château vividly illustrates the author's skill in working so artfully with an intricate plot as to make it appear simple. The play is Anouilh's version of *Pygmalion* and *My Fair Lady:* his purpose in confronting the high society of the château with the lowly Isabelle is to demonstrate that an insignificant ballerina can appear to be the attractive niece of an *homme du monde* to those who wish to see her that way, nothing but a vulgar, earthy girl to others, and a nonentity to herself. The "truth" of Isabelle's identity varies according to the persons whom she encounters, and Horace—who is playing a game of split personality —is in a position to mock those seeking in vain to discover this "truth."

Horace, who organizes the ball in order to teach the outrageously spoiled Diana a lesson about life, is determined to upset the "normal order"—this evening Diana, for a change, will not be allowed to triumph, will not be the belle of the ball; Isabelle, instead, will be the center of attraction. Although Horace finds that he must do a great deal of improvising in his presentation of Isabelle, since she is much more "conventional" than he had expected her to be, the difficulty of the task only increases his spirit of combat. The episodes which are inevitable when the poor come into direct contact with the wealthy on hostile territory aid Horace considerably in his challenge of the established order. When, for example, Diana's father, a modern Croesus, bribes Isabelle to leave the château so that his daughter will have no competition, and she replies that she is leaving without taking his handsome bribe, he protests that it is "not in the order of things." [1]

Isabelle is, of course, the heroine of both the evening and the play. It is she who assumes her role in Horace's comedy with the greatest ease and naturalness, for the poor are well-trained in games of escape. When, finally, her identity is revealed, she slips comfortably back into her true self, cognizant that her invitation to the château is not of long duration: "My role is finished, the curtain falls, and I am leaving." [2] Frédéric has fallen in love with her, however, and the "pink" play ending demands that they live happily ever after. Subsequent events are even "pinker," for Diana becomes a pauper (owing to a financial crash in which her father loses all of his money), permitting Horace to love her for her beauty alone. The final curtain is appropriately "pinkissimo," for Anouilh allows Diana's father's money to be returned to him, doubled in amount.

II Cécile

Less intricate is the plot of *Cécile, ou l'Ecole des pères*. Araminthe, Cécile's governess and companion, has assured the farcical Monsieur Orlas, Cécile's very strict father, that Cécile (who is planning to elope that very evening) would no sooner marry her lover than she, Araminthe, would marry him (Monsieur Orlas). However, after the execution of a plan conceived by Araminthe —a plan replete with confusion and mistaken identity—the two pairs of lovers are united.

The main interest of this play is in the gallery of portraits created by Anouilh and in the theatricality of the contrived happy ending. Cécile is a sweet, demure, and unsophisticated young lady of seventeen in love with a swashbuckling chevalier; he is an ungenerous young man who hopes that his father will, by putting his three sisters into convents, transfer their dowries to him so that he will have enough money to marry the not-so-wealthy Cécile. The chevalier's notion that his sisters are too ugly to know love is a theme that appears frequently in Anouilh's plays,[3] and also has its autobiographical elements. The chevalier's father is typically concerned with the dimensions of his future daughter-in-law's dowry: no sooner had the chevalier obtained his first kiss from Cécile, than his father obtained from Monsieur Orlas's accountant the most exact information on his financial status.

Cécile's father is a bourgeois widower who admittedly has never done a day's work in his life. He expresses his love for Araminthe through such vulgarities as caressing her knee under the table and knocking on her door at night. Determined to save his daughter's honor by foiling the chevalier's discovered plan to elope with her, he posts himself in the garden under her window, armed and draped in a gray cape and with the taste for blood in his mouth. This melodramatic situation has been planned by Araminthe to facilitate Monsieur Orlas's declarations of love for her.

Araminthe, Cécile's twenty-three-year-old governess, is a schemer and an improviser, similar to Horace in L'Invitation au Château. Her intrigues provide the deux ex machina for the play's happy dénouement: with a clap of her hands, a wedding cake, already inscribed with the names of Cécile and the chevalier, Araminthe and Monsieur Orlas, appears, making the respective marriages a fait accompli.

Despite the seemingly happy ending, Anouilh's "black" philosophy in matters of marriage is reflected in Cécile's final words in the play. Turning to her lover she somberly comments: "I shall make you suffer"[4]—an echo of Monsieur Orlas's earlier observation that lovers always hurt each other cruelly, and also a presage of the tragic relationships between lovers in the next two "brilliant" plays, La Répétition, ou l'Amour puni and Colombe.

III La Répétition

La Répétition is perhaps the best example of Anouilh's construction of a play within a play. Tigre, a wealthy Count eager to escape the tedious reality of his life, decides to stage a production of Marivaux's *La Double Inconstance* at a banquet: the diners will be the actors and the spectators will be forced to hear them to the end of the meal. Unaware that his wife and friends cannot understand his illusory escape, the Count tends to abuse them by treating them as his puppets, and further incurs their rancor by falling in love with Lucile, a poor young woman in his employ as the governess of twelve orphans that are being raised in a wing of the château.

Because aristocratic society cannot accept romantic purity, the lords and ladies invent implausible schemes to exile Lucile, who has inspired in the jaded Count a love outside of time and circumstance, beyond good and evil. Héro, the Count's usually inebriated friend, finally "persuades" her to leave by alluding to Tigre's supposed infidelity; he then seduces the heartbroken Lucile. The despondent Count sets out on a hopeless search for her, with the Countess predicting that her husband will have forgotten about Lucile in two months and will start a new escapade. Héro, his propensity for smashing things having been fully expressed by this act of shattering Lucile, taunts the Countess' lover into challenging him to a duel that is, in effect, suicide.

This "brilliant" play is delicately and scintillatingly fashioned around the "black" theme of the destruction of a pure love, and on graceful shiftings between the reality of Tigre's love and the illusion of Marivaux's play, which tells of an ugly duckling brought into a princely household inhabited by *commedia dell'arte* characters. Just as there is a separation of "races" among the *commedia* characters (Harlequin vs. Flaminia and Lisette), at the château Lucile is separated from Héro, the noble alcoholic, and from the rich and noble *ménage à quatre*: the Countess, her ridiculous lover Villebosse, the Count, and his hypocritical mistress Hortensia. Hortensia tries to dissuade Tigre from taking seriously his love for the plebeian Lucile by appealing sensually to his class instincts: "You are of another race. . . . Your head, your heart, may do a thousand foolish things, but your hands rarely make a mistake. I am sure you still desire me." [5]

The scenes that Lucile witnesses at the château serve to strengthen her pride in her "race" and to entrench her more firmly in the code of honor of the poor. The Countess and Hortensia, neither of whom truly loves the Count, scheme to destroy Tigre's and Lucile's love solely to gratify their own egos. Hortensia would recapture him from Lucile simply to satisfy her pride that he has not abandoned her for a nonentity; the Countess would take him back simply to get rid of Villebosse, who bores her. The Countess' plan to lose one of her rings and then to search for it in all of the rooms of the château including Lucile's, in the hope that this will force the governess into leaving, indicates the dignity, honor, and sensitivity that even the rich associate with the "poor" race.

The Count (who bears similarities to Anouilh himself) recognizes that only the "poor" race produces geniuses and heroes, while the rich spend their lives taking futility seriously.[6] He nevertheless sees in his class some signs of talent, and would like to believe that he is one of its talented representatives. The Count has, in fact, the makings of a hero: in 1940 he alone, with a small makeshift cannon, resisted a storm of Pomeranian grenadiers. The fact that he has elements of both races renders him a tragic figure with a split personality.

Deep inside himself, the Count knows that he is not a hero. He is absorbed in his own game of futility, and although he enjoys thinking of himself as a genius in order to excuse his irritability with the "actors" who are rehearsing the Marivaux play, he knows that he is not a genius either. His words to the Countess recall those of the Count in La Grotte and the Prince in Léocadia: "No one asks our class to produce geniuses. We aren't fortunate enough to have earned that pleasure; we leave such bonuses to the people, who can produce a million clodhoppers every three or four generations, and can bring forth triumphantly a top-honors student or a President of the Republic. All that is asked of our class is to be coherent and durable. We all have talent, and it lasts throughout the centuries. We do what we can." [7]

The Count seems to sense that the insufficiencies of his person and his lack of greatness might be rectified by an experience analogous to his heroism in the face of the German attack: pure love might reproduce the happiness he felt at that time, and might inspire the same reactions of courage and elation. Lucile proves that he is correct, for as soon as they realize that they are in love, everything around the Count falls into place, everything becomes simple and peaceful, as though he had defied death itself.

The first three acts of the play, then, are "brilliant" variations on a theme. The fourth act, however, brings the loss of Lucille, who has been victimized by the cruel inhabitants of the château; her disappearance causes the symbolic death of Tigre, and the revelation of her purity leads Héro to invite his own actual death. The play ends in bitterness and blackness, setting the tone for the last of the *pièces brillantes, Colombe,* where once again a corrupt society ultimately subjugates the heroic.

IV   Colombe

Julien, the defiant son of actress Madame Alexandra, has married Colombe, a young flower vendor. His mother detests him and loves her other son, Armand, who flatters her and is slave to her every whim. When Julien is drafted he entrusts Colombe and their child to the care of his vituperative mother. Madame Alexandra offers her daughter-in-law bit parts in her plays; gradually Colombe succumbs to the sordid environment of the theatrical world and becomes Armand's mistress. Julien returns from the war and learns of his wife's deceit.

In the closing scene, Julien's cryptic words, "Now the story is beginning," suggest that an illusion-in-the-making may enable the hero to escape horrible reality, but Anouilh's penchant for irony leads him to end the play in a flashback of Julien's and Colombe's first meeting, when the two vowed eternal love. Despite the sincerity of this vow, eternity has no place in the affairs of men, and time, as Anouilh has shown elsewhere, can be no more than a relative thing.

Julien is another male *"sauvage."* According to his family, sudden calm possessed their home when he abandoned them two years earlier. He hates his past, symbolized by his mother, and tries to shed it when he enters into marriage with Colombe, describing himself as an "orphan." He attempts to erase the memory of his early childhood, when his mother put him up at the cold and frugal home of a miserly soup merchant (who lived twenty miles outside Paris). She did not visit her son for six months, and when, as a publicity stunt, she finally decided to pay him a visit together with some photographers, they were unable to take his picture, so thin and scabby had he become. Madame Alexandra had caused her husband to commit suicide three weeks after their marriage, having deserted him for her troupe's leading actor. From his father, Julien has inherited rigor, probity, and honesty as well as streaks of sullen anger, silence, nastiness and misanthropy. He describes the rest of humanity as ugly, weak, and either stupid or wicked. He hates all men and associates them with the wounds which he has received in life.

Julien's cynicism is almost as strong as that of Lucien in *Roméo et Jeannette*. When called into the army, he sarcastically says that he is going to defend the Republic. He then explains that he is an anti-militarist who has no patriotic feelings whatever, yet he refuses to ask his mother to have him deferred. He considers it "ugly" to try to get out of military duty, even though he loves and will miss Colombe. His strong sense of honesty prevents him from draft-dodging ("I want to be able to look at my face in the mirror when I shave").[8] Quite different from Julien is his brother Armand, who hides behind his mother's skirts and obtains all that he desires through flattery. Julien needs his mother's help, but to all admonitions that flies are not caught with vinegar, Julien retorts that he has no sugar on him.

Colombe is subjected to Julien's scrupulous code of morality: she is obliged to stay at home to read serious books and to cultivate a taste for Mozart and Beethoven, and she is forbidden to dance and indulge in small talk. Julien's standards, however, are far too high for his wife, and as soon as he leaves for the army she falls into little laxities such as opening the door to the mailman in her slip, and bathing in front of an open window without worrying about the man next door. She rebels against the strictness which Julien has imposed upon her, not out of love, but for himself, for the sake of satisfying the demands of his principles. He has not wanted Colombe as his wife simply because she loved him, but rather because she swore that she would be his wife; love to him was secondary to the oath.

After learning of Colombe's deception, Julien cruelly forces his brother to kiss him on the lips so he can know what effect it could possibly have had on Colombe. Disgusted and disconcerted, he wipes his mouth with the back of his hand, without having attained any clearer comprehension of what pleasure his wife has found in Armand. Moreover, Julien cannot understand how Colombe could have greeted him with such affection and love on his twenty-four-hour leaves, and then shared Armand's bed. It does not occur to him that his search for truth is not the prevailing preoccupation of other mortals, and that hypocrisy requires less effort than probity.

The pure image of his wife, Colombe tells Julien, is a figment of his imagination. She does not really exist, for she, Colombe, is just a woman, and all she knows how to do is give pleasure. Julien, although he persists in preserving his memory of an ideal Colombe, also loves her as a woman. He chose to relinquish the masculine liberty that would have allowed him to cross the oceans with his comrades and pick up girls in every port. His love for her offered him enough adventures. He will keep forever that image of the Colombe he loved, refusing to let his wife soil that memory with stories of her sordid life as a flower vendor.

Julien runs to his mother to tell her how much he loved *that* Colombe and how much he will always love her. Madame Alexandra tries to open his eyes, telling him that nothing is "forever," that everything in life changes, including feelings and sentiments. She suggests that he cease trying to be a pelican offering his entrails to humanity—that in the long run the world gets disgusted and does not want any more "food" forced down its throat. Julien must understand, his mother tells him, that Colombe would now like to change menus. Julien's answer to his mother preserves the image of *her* that he has in his mind: an old rat in a cheese; a mother hen hatching a safe full of gold. All of the "brilliance" of Madame Alexandra cannot outshine the tragic splendor of Julien's Catonian steadfastness.

CHAPTER 6

Pièces grinçantes

THE "jarring" plays are in some ways similar to the "black" plays, but now Anouilh has shifted his attention from the "heroic race" to the "mediocre race" and its compromise with life. The effect of these plays is "jarring" because two irreconcilables— comedy and tragedy—clash on a battlefield strewn with the cast-off armor of humanity's defense mechanisms.

One critic has considered the *pièces grinçantes* as more than the playing with a tragicomic situation.[1] He sees the plots as suppurations of wounds and the characters as embodiments of hatred, as life's failures, with no hope of redemption. We should, however, read into the *pièces grincantes* an intensification of cynicism, together with a certain tolerance of the unsuccessful hero. The rigid philosophy of the earlier plays yields to the mellowing influence of maturity. Anouilh, now relieved of financial pressures and savoring the luxury of leisure and worldwide acclaim, seems resigned to the ineluctability of love's impurity and the evanescence of ideals.

The central character in these plays is a middle-aged man (the General, the Count, Ornifle) striving to remain young, blossoming every spring like an old tree, but a tree whose trunk is rotting. His life is absurd; his ideas are reactionary. Plagued by conscience, he recognizes the purity and beauty of intransigence when he sees it, but is incapable of correcting his own loose morals and weaknesses.

I Ardèle

Ardèle, ou la Marguerite (1948) is a vaudeville farce that leads to tragic consequences. General Saint-Pé, his life for years governed by an invalid wife, is disconcerted by the love affair that has blossomed between his hunchbacked sister Ardèle and the hunchbacked tutor of his ten-year-old son, Toto. He dismisses the tutor, locks his sister in her room, and calls for a family conference to discuss and hopefully to ameliorate the situation. By this time Ardèle, who remains invisible throughout the play, has locked her door from within and has gone on a hunger strike.

In a futile attempt to convince Ardèle of the "scandalous and immoral" nature of her actions, the family members take turns in embarking upon specious yet revealing homilies on the subject of love. The General and his brother-in-law, the Count, expound upon the absurdity of her conduct and of the principle of dying for love. To Ardèle's demand that the people on the other side of her door explain *their* conduct, the Count (Anouilh's spokesman and the "middle-hero" of the play) responds that they behave as well as their concept of duty and their lack of courage permit them to.

The young and idealistic Nicolas, oldest son of the General, is the only person wholly sympathetic toward Ardèle and genuinely ashamed of the General and his entourage. He encourages his aunt to resist the arguments of her tormentors, to stand firm and protest against those who would destroy true love, such as his for Nathalie and Ardèle's for the tutor. He shouts to his aunt to love against everyone's will, and to do so with all her might.

At some time during this inundation of advice, Ardèle's door is accidentally left unlocked. That evening, her lover slips into her room and the two commit suicide, escaping the pressures of the outside world but simultaneously destroying their fragile love. The type of "love" that persists, however, is depicted by Anouilh through the grotesque and ironic game played by Toto and Marie-Christine, his ten-year-old cousin. Garbed as adults, the two are simulating what to them is a typical adult love scene. Each one insisting that his love is greater and deeper than the other's, they begin to argue the point, ending up on the floor cursing and beating each other as the curtain falls.

General Saint-Pé is a ridiculous bungler and the epitome of compromise. He conceives the acceptance of Ardèle's love as equivalent to disruption and disorder in the Establishment. To reestablish order all that is needed is to approach the situation in terms of force: they must force the locked door open, force food down Ardèle's throat, force her to resume her piano playing and force her to forget about her lover. When confronting the tutor with arguments intended to dissuade and confound him, the Gen-

eral puts on his uniform and all his decorations to inspire within
himself the feeling that he is a superman. He is chagrined to discover that the tutor is a man, in spite of his hump, and that he is
"savage" enough to refuse the salary to which he is entitled upon
dismissal.

The General has felt his old age more intensely since the arrival
in his home of his twenty-year-old daughter-in-law, Nathalie, who
is like a breath of fresh air in the household. So impressed is he
with her purity that he prays to God he will never merit her scorn.
Unfortunately, his prayer was uttered on a Sunday, when God
was probably too busy to hear him; the General, realizing that
Nathalie can never respect him in his ridiculousness, consoles
himself by making love to the chambermaid.

Nathalie, however, has also made concessions and compromises. Originally an orphaned *"sauvage,"* comparable to Adèle in
La Grotte, she was brought up in poverty and made to suffer and
be insulted because she was living on her aunt's money. Nathalie
decided to marry Nicolas' brother Maxime in order to be near
Nicolas whom she really loves but who is too young yet to marry.
The ideal, secret love between Nathalie and her brother-in-law is
shattered when she admits that she enjoys physical love with her
husband.

The General's sister (the Countess), her husband (the Count),
and her lover (Villardieu) form the eternal triangle in which the
lover is a member of the household, is jealous of the Count and
resents the husband's compliments to his own wife. Villardieu defends his position as a matter of honor; it is *his* honor that matters,
not the Count's. He is intolerant of the Countess' compassion for
her husband when he loses at baccarat, and cannot bear to see her
dance with the Count twice in succession. He is miserable because
of his suspicion that the Countess may still be in love with her
husband, and spends his nights watching the bedroom door of the
Count, who sleeps alone, in fear that he may have a secret rendez-
vous with his own wife.

What saves the Count from appearing ridiculous is his ability to
recognize the grotesqueness of his own situation. For this reason,
he is quite tolerant and understanding of the love between the
hunchbacks and views it simply as another disorder among the
disorders of the world. He champions the logic of Ardèle's doing
as she pleases, just as the rest of the household exercises its right

to live as it will. The Count goes even so far as to suggest that perhaps Ardèle knows something about a kind of love that they, the non-hunchbacks, know nothing about.

The long dialogue between the Count and the General on the subject of love reveals the latter's simple thinking: love is short-lived, and then you pay dearly for the rest of your life; peaceful couples in love are nonexistent. The Count is cynical on the subject: love is like war; it causes men and women to fight tooth and nail. Once the battle has started, all is fair, and one must kill the other. An escape for the Count from his unsuccessful marriage has been his affair with a young seamstress—also invisible throughout the play—who, on several occasions, has taken poison in desperation but has been saved each time by the prompt action of the Count. Her love for him is pure, as is the love of the other invisible characters[2] in the play.

Another secondary character, the General's wife, has been driven to insanity by her love. Ever since she first met her husband, she has been spying on him and resenting his passion for every woman he looks at, as well as those he imagines while making love to her. She would like to penetrate into the sanctuary of his mind, where immorality has free reign. For ten years her insanity has prevented her from sleeping at night because she is aware of couples making love all about her: in the room next to hers (which happens to be Ardèle's), in nature, among the peacocks, the insects, and the flowers. She is determined to stop the process of lovemaking, if not in nature, at least in her own home. Frenziedly, she demands that the lovemaking in the room adjacent to hers be stopped. Thus, unknowingly, she is a pathetic accomplice in the suppression of a pure love—the same kind of love that drove her to irrationality. It is only the General's "conscience" that prevents him from abandoning his pitiful wife altogether, and it is his lack of courage that drives him into his affair with the maid.

The three generations of "impure" lovers in *Ardèle* (the General and his wife and the Countess and Villardieu, Nicolas and Nathalie, and the battling ten-year-olds, Toto and Marie-Christine) are reminiscent of Armand Salacrou's generations in *Sens interdit*.[3] Both authors caricature the bourgeoisie as bored masses, seeking escape from tedium through immorality, and unconcerned with the search for a truth that might give absolute meaning to their lives. Both demonstrate that "bourgeois love" is adulterous and empty, while purity is impermanent and intangible. Ardèle, the symbol of pure love, is neither seen nor heard, and she is ultimately destroyed.

II   La Valse des Toréadors

After the curtain had fallen on *Ardèle,* Anouilh's sense of continuity in the game of life caused it to rise again on *La Valse des Toréadors* (1951), in which the banal existence of General Saint-Pé and his wife, Amélie, is continued. The General is still at the mercy of a wife who now feigns paralysis in order to keep her husband close to her. He is still obsessed with women; she is still obsessed with his obsession. Although Amélie does not love the General, she considers him her "property," something belonging to her alone, and refuses to forfeit her claim.

The couple is visited by Ghislaine de Sainte-Euverte, a woman the General had fallen in love with seventeen years ago and who has been waiting for him to marry her since that time. Soon after her arrival, however, she falls in love with Gaston, his secretary. Furious, the General attempts to prevent their marriage by requiring the consent of Gaston's parents, since he is a minor. As fate and farce will have it, Gaston turns out to be the General's illegitimate son. The General must resign himself to a vacuous life of serving his wife and sleeping with his servants.

Throughout the play, Anouilh has manipulated his characters through interludes of mistaken identity and mass confusion, but comic relief, however clever and amusing, cannot lighten the tragedy that is the General's life. He is alone and afraid, and although his search for some "tiny bit of happiness" is inane, he knows that it is part of the role he must play if he wishes to survive his degradation.

Since his marriage, life for the General has been a series of reproaches, scratches, slaps, sobs, broken plates, suicide attempts, and reconciliations, followed by another "love" cycle. To make his life bearable, he cherishes the memory of Ghislaine, with whom he had danced the Waltz of the Toreadors at a ball seventeen years earlier. The family doctor, who understands that the General is wasting away his life by living in the past, suggests to him that he cut off his past before gangrene sets in, that he hurry to gather his rosebuds in the little time left him. To the doctor's query as to why he does not marry Ghislaine, the General, recipient of many military rewards for heroism and of eighteen wounds in battle, replies, "I am a coward. . . . I can't see people suffer . . ." [4] just as he had explained in *Ardèle* why he could not leave his wife.

Relations between the General and his wife are as inimical as possible, even though each is genuinely concerned about the other's survival. Offense and insults have replaced marital love. To the General's defense of his extramarital relations "to prove he is still a man," Amélie protests that women, too, would like to prove they are still women, that her love letters to the doctor and to her past lovers have helped her to do so, while her husband has played the fool by waiting seventeen years for Mademoiselle de Sainte-Euverte. Amélie mocks her husband's concept of woman's honor as the defense of the integrity of the household, of the family name and of the children, to which the General responds by accusing his wife of being the daughter of a "kept" woman and a venal acrobat, which explains her loose morals.

If Amélie regards her husband as chattel, as her personal "garbage-can," the General feels his wife to be an albatross around his neck: he will never be able to cast her off; their names will be engraved together on their tombstone. Their scenes are especially depressing and tragic for we know that no matter how deep the offenses are, the couple is inseparable. Amélie and the General will never shed each other, just as their pasts can never be shed. No matter how much they hurt each other, they will not leave each other.

Amélie knows that even though the General may make promises to others and keep those promises for seventeen years, he will always be hers. The macabre is achieved when she forces him to dance the Waltz of the Toreadors with her, Amélie, his old skeleton, his wife, his remorse. At this point the irrational General attempts to choke his wife to death, but his cowardice quickly repossesses him and he cannot fulfill his desire. Ironically, the gesture revives a spark of love in Amélie, for the operatic scene has convinced her that their love must indeed be great.

The General's misery is intensified by his view of life as a split second between "too young to know" and too old to do anything but write one's memoirs, and by the introversion that causes him to look inside of himself and, finding no one, to turn outward; he reassures himself by making a fanfare, covering his "shell" with oak clusters and other decorations, but he knows always, in Pascalian terms, that he is alone and that he is afraid of his solitude.

Physically, the General is as flabby as he is morally. When Ghislaine reveals to him that she has in her possession some love letters signed by his wife and addressed to the doctor (whose visits, incidentally, invariably make Amélie feel considerably better), the General's "honor" demands the doctor's blood. A hilarious play on "blood" and "blood pressure" ensues, as the General threatens to slap the doctor in provocation of a duel. The doctor threatens to slap back; the two mentally compare their respective ranks in the local sports society, and finally lower their trousers to compare the solidity of their bellies. The General realizes that the doctor clearly has the advantage over him, and the subject of the duel is dismissed.

The General's wretchedness is even further intensified by his two ugly, ungraceful daughters, Estelle and Sidonie. He foresees that it will not be easy to marry them off in a day and age when even second lieutenants, as all other men, want dowries and beauty from their fiancées. Estelle and Sidonie are in love with Gaston and when, to their great chagrin, they learn that Gaston loves Ghislaine, they run away from home, leaving behind a letter declaring that their suffering is too great for them to continue living.

The General is not the least worried about his daughters, for he knows that they are too ugly to commit suicide. The doctor corroborates the General's feelings by recalling that, in life, young women die of the same sicknesses as old men, and that ugly ducklings who threaten suicide are recurrent characters in life's *commedia dell'arte*. As predicted, Estelle and Sidonie, having swum out to the middle of the suicide pond, turn around and swim back and then go home to discover that Gaston is their brother. Estelle's ingenuous "Why didn't Mother know about it?" adds to the general distress.

Estelle and Sidonie have obviously learned their dramatic gestures from their mother, a frequent victim of ludicrous crises of jealousy and suicide attempts which are "jarring" rather than heroic, as in the *pièces noires*. Amélie's feigned paralysis is pathetic. When, however, that paralysis vanishes long enough for her to run out of her bedroom threatening suicide, and the doctor and the

General run after her, one in the direction of the railroad tracks and the other in the direction of the pond; when Ghislaine attempts to shoot herself with a little pistol that does not fire, and refuses the pond or the railroad tracks in order not to die with her rival—then we are witnessing true farce, climaxed by Ghislaine's dramatic act of jumping out of a window onto Gaston, who is lying in a hammock below. He is forced to fondle and kiss her to revive her, and is caught in the act by the General.

When all the suicide-threatening ladies have succumbed to the sedative administered by the doctor, a dialogue ensues on the subject of women and on the definition of the soul. On the first subject the doctor and the General are in agreement: the natural state of women is either to bear suffering and maladies or, if they should stop suffering, to inflict it on men, who always remain little boys and never have all of the ills that beset women. The doctor then distinguishes between the introverted nature of the man, who tends to relate things to his inner self, and the woman's tendency to project outwards and to express herself through others. According to the doctor, unhappy is the man upon whom the extroverted woman chooses to pounce.

When the General asks why medicine does not find a way to make women sleep all the time (except a little at night), the materialistic side of the doctor replies that women are necessary for the orderly running of households, for frying eggs and washing dishes. On the other hand, to the General's question of why we complicate life by forbidding men free love with buxom maids, the doctor's spiritualistic side answers: "Because we have a soul, General. Believe this old freethinker. It's our soul that poisons us. The underskirts of a maid are fine for a moment, but then . . . without love, without true desire, what emptiness! And then the soul comes to fill that emptiness, and your mouth is full of it, and it comes out through your nose. It's disgusting." [5] The General protests that this feeling is not disgusting, that on the contrary it creates a swell of idealism after a contraction of disgust. A base and ugly act is a necessary form of voluptuousness that inspires an opposite feeling of man's nobility: the secret moment of ignominy is followed by scruples, good resolutions, reading of good books, walks in nature, and a symphony of idealistic thoughts.

This ingenious balance may be equated with the virtue of Anouilh's pseudo-hero: for him, virtue is equal to a moment of ignominy plus scruples, idealism, and good resolutions. The equation explains the ease with which the General can make love to the maids, and why he never took Ghislaine as his mistress or left his wife to marry her. The element "virtue" is equal to conscience and honor.

According to the General it is the soul that creates the harmony and equilibrium of the equation, and his search for peace of soul must include the ignoble act. His quest for this peace in maids' petticoats is comparable to Héro's similar search in the bottoms of whiskey glasses (*La Répétition*). Each man's definition of what is beautiful, what is inspiring, what brings peace and tranquility to him, cannot be found in museums, nor is each man a sculptor or a painter in his own right. Therefore, according to the General, each man must create his own beauty and provide a very personal interpretation of the elements of his virtue equation. Relativity, not absoluteness, is the standard to be applied.

In the scene following the "soul purification" dialogue the General tests his meaning of honor on Gaston. To demonstrate the element of ignominy in honor, he reminds Gaston of the fable of the Spartan youth who stole a fox, hid it under his tunic, and preferred to have the fox eat his stomach rather than admit the theft. Honor demands keeping up appearances, even though the flesh is weak.

Gaston's readiness to die for the sake of honor and ideals reminds the General of his youth. Nostalgically recalling his military days of non-compromise, he murmurs agreement: "You are right, my boy, it is ignoble to grow old and understand." [6] Yet he teaches Gaston the grand lesson of compromise simply because he, the General, cannot be a true hero or make others suffer, for any reason whatsoever. His counsel to Gaston is to find a true companion who will struggle with him to obtain his goal. Once again the concept of the ideal "bisexual" woman, a silent, tender "comrade" fighting side by side with a man during the day and then transforming herself into a woman at night, is stressed.

To the General's subsequent chagrin, Gaston takes his words—and Ghislaine—to heart. Feeling empty and buffoonish, the General's only resort is to don his full military attire, seize two old and rusted swords from the wall and challenge Gaston to a duel. The doctor, however, has only to suggest the strains of the Waltz of the Toreadors for the General to put down his sword.

After the *deus ex machina* in the form of the discovery of Gaston's parents provides the denouement of the play, the General, in utter abjection, turns from everyone in the realization that it is now too late for him to live, or love, or give his heart to anyone else. His eyes turn to the new, buxom maid who has just entered his wife's service, as he reflects that it is only imbeciles who think they have souls. As he attempts to seduce the maid in a darkened room, his mind turns to his inner self: "We'll feel less alone, in the dark. . . ." [7] The defeated General is left in a complete void, deserted even by his philosophy of the soul, as the curtain falls on *La Valse des Toréadors.*

III   L'Hurluberlu

Eight years after *La Valse des Toréadors,* our spirited General returns to the front lines of life's battle in *L'Hurluberlu, ou le Réactionnaire amoureux.* [8] The significance of the subtitle is that the hero is in love with France, and expresses his love in terms of the rejection of Newton's discoveries, progress and innovation, and psychology as a new science to explain human weakness. He seeks to restore imagination and poetry to the hearts of his countrymen, for he believes that scientific precision masks nine-tenths of the truth.

Now married to a woman twenty years younger than himself and living in the midst of a grotesque and inane society that bores his wife, the General provides her with the means to lead a brilliant social life in their home, which has become the cover-up for his secret campaign to rid France of her corruption. His efforts to distract his wife and his plots for the restoration of French good sense and virtue are both doomed to failure, but his dreams and his ideals are as pure as a child's, making him lovable in spite of his "hurluberluism."

The General is finally forced to face realities: that his wife will undoubtedly one day take a lover; that his daughter, who falls in love every five months, has this time allowed herself to be seduced and then abandoned by a young man of the "new generation" who knows nothing about concepts of honor, duty, virtue, and loyalty; that his fellow conspirators are one by one deserting him. The rigid, uncompromising, reactionary old General, after all his attempts to save civilization, is brutally knocked to the ground, first by his older daughter's unrepentant seducer and again by the milkman, whose son the General had slapped for improper behavior toward his younger daughter.

From his down-and-out position the General reaches for a bite of "*mininistatfia*," which he shares with his small son, Toto, whom he now takes into his confidence: they will go into combat, just like Joan of Arc, insignificant humans, weaker than their adversaries, hoping that God is on their side and playing their roles in life's marionette show. When Toto asks whether the play will always be serious, the General answers that the tragedy is always the same but that man, an inconsolable and gay animal, will always be able to laugh.

The General's obsession, which subsequently led to his brutal recall to reality, was his vision of France as a wounded thoroughbred about to die in the pangs of childbirth while her children, the human race, stand about helplessly, wondering whether to change cars this year and figuring how to defraud the tax bureau. The General is outraged by the spinelessness of contemporary Frenchmen, by their constant search for more pleasures and comforts in life. He is irritated by the groveling morality of the modern man who has everything produced for him without any efforts of his own: art, music, sports, etc. are served to him, and when he gets old, wrinkles are removed from his face for him.

The challenges of rigorous application and perseverance, which made France great and glorious and beautiful in the past, and the austerity once practiced by French peasants and workers, have now been lost. The young generation is bored and boorish, disrespectfully using first names, familiarity, and slang in speaking with elders. The General has decided to organize a strategic campaign against the list of corrupting worms drawn up by his friend Ledadu, a hardware merchant, whose pet "worm" is the replacement of good old pots and pans by modern ceramics and plastics. The General's fifth column is not a mass movement, for he believes that the future is in the hands of an "effective minority." His efforts have earned him the title of the "dirty fascist in town."

The General's long-standing confidant, the family doctor, shows much more lucidity in analyzing history and in suggesting that his friend abandon his hopeless plan. The doctor, unconvinced of the soundness of the General's strategy and of Ledadu's ideas from the point of view of economics and marketing, claims that his many maternity cases keep him busy at night and prevent him from working with the underground. The doctor defends modern corporations on the grounds that without them we would be regressing two thousand years in history. The General, however, dismisses the doctor's ideas about the "ineluctable course of history" as nonsense, and maintains that perhaps we ought to regress two thousand years if we are on the wrong track. Nature, argues the General, at times goes back in her evolutionary process, giving up a tail or an eye that may prove to be useless.

The General also sincerely believes that a handful of men *can* change events. Such men are not those government officials who puff themselves up as heroes even though they have caused two national bankruptcies and have lost face in a war.[9] They are rather those modest, dutiful men whose individual acts serve to create a solid foundation for society. The General tells the Curé, who would like, in a sermon, to cite the General as an admirable father, that there are no admirable fathers: the pelican that nourishes his children with his own entrails and the soldier who goes to battle are doing nothing more than their strict duty; they deserve no medals. For the General, fathers are at the head of their families for the same reason that kings are at the head of their kingdoms: they have the right to spank but, at the same time, the duty to inspire authority by manifesting exceptional talent and virtue. Unless children can consider their fathers heroes, the world's equilibrium is lost.

The General's sense of honor, in the tradition of the butler in *La Grotte,* admits of no relaxation: no matter how absurd a concept of honor or duty may be, it must be adhered to inflexibly. The General is intolerant of his friend Lebellac who has violated the code of honor that applies to unmarried women of the upper class: Lebellac has kissed the General's spinster sister while they were in the kitchen together making pancakes. Lebellac ascribes his conduct to his "tenderness:" "a woman who falls into my arms causes me to fall in turn." [10] The General's rigor admits of no tenderness. Lebellac is scratched from the list of honorable conspirators.

The General is also intolerant of the theater because, on stage, God's creatures impudently mimic passions that they do not actually feel, and he is of the conviction that the price of such irreverence should be the excommunication of actors and actresses. He is intolerant of modern jazz trumpets that are blown for purposes other than reveille, taps, and calls to battle. For the General, life should be regulated by ordinances as precise as those in military manuals of instruction. He is as inflexible as the handful of Germans who even today try to cultivate Prussian traditions and Prussian virtues of the past—simplicity, modesty, incorruptibility, reliability, and a sense of duty and honor.

In the intimacy of his relations with his wife, Aglae, the General confesses to his own grotesqueness, but admits that he cannot make himself over; he recognizes that his fits of anger, his idiosyncrasies, and his rigidity annoy her, yet he maintains that rigor is a virtue which often requires that others suffer. Aglae loves her husband because he is just the opposite of her father, a facile and weak man. She reveals that she will not deceive her husband, not because she loves him, but only because she loves truth and because she has sworn not to deceive him. In her desire always to be truthful, when and if she falls in love with another man she will tell her husband and then leave with the man she loves. The General (quite the opposite of Julien, who wanted Colombe to remain his wife always *just* because she had vowed to) insists that only love must prevent her from deceiving him.

Aglae reproaches the General for his inflexibility in desiring things to be as he thinks they ought to be: she, France, human nature—all have to be hard, eternal, beautiful, and pure. Whenever he sees anything becoming corrupted he becomes frightfully angry, without realizing that everything on this earth changes. Aglae suggests that her husband come down to earth and face reality. Instead of conspiring, she suggests that he be pleasant and make compromises, and thereby be a little happier. The General is incapable of taking his wife's advice: his feigned pleasantness turns out to be sarcasm; his "happiness" turns out to be hypocrisy.

At the other end of the spectrum from the General—and symbolizing everything the reactionary detests—scintillates David Edward Mendigalès, a young progressive in search of excitement, a promoter of avant-garde, anti-Giraudoux, and anti-Claudel anti-dramas, in which characters do not speak, nothing happens for a very long time and the stage sets are limited to a bidet. After David Edward seduces and abandons the General's daughter, the General calls him on the carpet in an attempt to make him understand the ignominious nature of his conduct. The scene is frightening, confusing, and overwhelming for the General: he finds himself in hostile territory where every element of his orderly code of honor is methodically destroyed by a young man who has never been exposed to any concept of duty or loyalty.

Moreover, David Edward Mendigalès is presumptuous enough to inform the General that he knows neither how to handle his wife nor how to raise his children. He suggests that the General give his son, Toto, who is suffering from complexes, ineptness, and rigidity, some lessons in flexibility and efficiency. He further informs the General that everyone is laughing at his "secret conspiracy," which will never change the great economic and demographic trends of tomorrow's world. He tells the General that he is a fool to care for his gardener's varicose veins, for the gardener detests him for his pitying attitude.

David Edward suggests that the General be more like his father, a modern plastics manufacturer who keeps his employees happy by allowing them to introduce motions adopted by majorities and by voting leftist, but who is never duped because he knows that today's pyramids are being built by the sweat of slaves. Only the vocabulary has changed. Finally, David Edward tells the General that it is his inactivity that is disturbing him psychologically, and that he will try to help by getting him an administrative job in his father's office. The General is devastated and humiliated by this tirade that opens the floodgates of time against him.

One by one the General's friends drop out of his conspiracy: they have all been stricken by the "spirit of the age"—one of those rare diseases in which antibiotics do not work. Even Belazor, the extreme conservative who lived completely in the past, with no running water or electricity in his home, bows out. The General has only his *"mininistatfia"* to fall back on. In today's world of compromise purists must topple with a jarring thud; their fall is ridiculous and anachronistic, for the age is not one of heroism.

IV   Ornifle

Like the General, Ornifle in *Ornifle, ou le Courant d'air* (1955) is a would-be hero who has compromised with life. Once the author of rich and provocative verse, he is now a waning Don Juan who prostitutes his verse and, to retaliate against life's disillusionments, has become completely corrupt. He wears a mask of grimaces and harsh cruelty to hide his suffering.

Ornifle hurts everyone around him: his tolerant and submissive wife, his scapegoat secretary, Supo, who has loved him for ten years, his friends, and his illegitimate son, Fabrice. After discovering the "soul," Ornifle begins to gain some insight into himself and those he has hurt, but eventually returning to his corrupt self he attempts to seduce Marguerite, Fabrice's fiancée. His nemesis comes during a rendezvous with one of his paramours: while the two are together in a hotel he dies of a heart attack—the modern version of Molière's visitation scene in *Don Juan*. Truth has triumphed, as Ornifle knew it would, only somewhat sooner than would have pleased him.

Ornifle, the hack poet who writes quick-selling couplets and labels these verses Rimbaud and Péguy in his own mind, is a cynic par excellence. He believes only two things: that two plus two are not equal to four, and that his conscience, embodied in his secretary Supo, is ugliness personified. His life is an exercise in taking futility seriously and in destroying all spiritual, poetic, and human values.

In his confessions to Father Dubaton, a priest whom Ornifle rewards with hymns for the parish children, he expresses his guilt for not having sinned enough and his sorrow for all of the sins he did *not* commit. The priest begs Ornifle to devote his poetic inspiration to the Catholic Church and to the redemption of his soul; Ornifle replies, as does the Count in *La Répétition,* that futility is the only thing worth taking seriously in life, and that the only men who are of any use on the face of this earth are those who have been able to amuse people, who have allowed them to forget death.

In vain does the priest show perfect honesty to Ornifle in an attempt to get him to mend his ways; he says some touching things about the perfume of sinners, he recognizes the mercenary aspects of the Church, and explains the necessity of obtaining without charge verses from poets for the gratification of congregations. Father Dubaton explains that even though priests may wear skirts they are not girls, but rather the garbage pails of humanity, who know more about humanity's sins than the worst pleasure-seekers. No amount of priestly comprehension, however, can prompt Ornifle to modify his desire to deceive, to hurt, and to sin.

Ornifle teaches his public relations managers that the way to prove he has poetic genius is by using journalistic techniques such as a double page in full color and an eye-catching cover as a substitute for inspiration. Ornifle's verses flow with ease: as he poses for photographers, commercial and religious rhymes resound and he is certain that abundant financial reward and priestly indulgences will shower down upon his effortless efforts.

Ornifle's "talent" as a poet is exceeded only by the physical gift he possesses to lend luster to pearls. Therefore, another source of income is the wearing against his body of pearls brought to him by all the pretty women of Paris with whom he takes his pleasures indiscriminately, for he is obsessed with his quest for *the* body beautiful. His moral philosophy is summed up in two points: take pleasure, unscrupulously, wherever it can be found, and when a woman no longer gives pleasure, look elsewhere. Nevertheless, Ornifle knows that he can never find happiness in the perfect body that has no soul inside it, and this is what attracts him to his wife's intelligence.

The kind and gentle Countess (similar to the General's wife in *L'Hurluberlu*) is tolerant of her husband's aberrations. She is resigned to the fact that, since her body is not perfect, she cannot retain her husband's admiration and therefore the pleasures of her soul are denied him. On the other hand, she is tormented by the strangeness and unjustness of the fact that her husband's physical and spiritual happiness depends upon a simple mathematical relationship—the measurements of the perfect body.

In his obsession with the perfect body, and because of his hatred for children—especially ones that might resemble him— Ornifle has driven to abortion or to suicide-attempts the many women (including his wife) he has made pregnant. He knows that for this, Heaven is preparing a thunderbolt to strike him, *à la Don Juan,* and that he will ultimately have to pay the price of his pleasures. The thought intensifies his cruelty, which is heaped mainly upon his devoted but ugly secretary Supo, who, at the end of the play, is driven to insanity by Ornifle's insults and outrages; in a moving soliloquy she maintains that she is beautiful, or at least that her body, which has been touched by no one, is beautiful. Her soul, which unfortunately shines in her face, is ugly and stinking. So devastating has Ornifle's influence on her been, that the pure, devoted, conscientious, and conscience-providing Supo has come to believe that beauty is ugliness.

The concept of the soul, which Ornifle has shut out of his mind since he began his search for physical pleasure, is still very much alive although suppressed in his conscience. He believes he gave his soul to his wife when they married, and, now that his health has been failing, he feels he needs his soul back for a while. His wife refuses his request on the grounds that Ornifle would now frighten his soul, which is no longer accustomed to him; she cannot offer her own soul because it has died—of hunger. This is the Countess' way of pleading eloquently for her husband's love, but, for Ornifle, love is to be found only in railroad-station novels. He thinks so highly of the Greek theater because there is not a single love scene in it.

In a fatalistic and bestial image of love, Ornifle compares men's loves to those of dogs on leashes:

We are like doggies dancing a little ballet of desire. I sniff you, you sniff me, I turn away, I turn back, I don't want any part of you, all right, I'll take you. And since I've accepted, it's for a lifetime. . . . And then someone (we don't know who) suddenly pulls at the leash and the doggie who was dreaming about eternity is snatched away . . . until chance, or the person who was walking him, thinking about his own affairs five feet above, unconsciously leads the doggie toward another doggie. Then the ballet starts all over again, with the same vows, until the next pull on the leash that again interrupts.

Ornifle is bored by and scornful of Mademoiselle Supo's declarations of love. He is cognizant that he can neither merit nor reciprocate his wife's love. He is resigned to the fact that true love, which takes pleasure in mutual renunciation, is charming but rare. Therefore he, Ornifle, with his theatrical sense, will step out of his role as a man and be a creator: he will pretend he is the person walking the dogs. He nobly leads his illegitimate son Fabrice into the arms of Marguerite, the daughter of Ornifle's literary rival, but as he forces the young couple to embrace, a fit of jealousy overcomes him. Rejecting his last chance for self-redemption, Ornifle now decides to go to the provinces with his son and future daughter-in-law, where he will "amuse himself" with Marguerite while Fabrice is studying at the university. Ornifle is engaging his immorality and his soul in a gamble against time: "Men do many things . . . that God does not want. He won the first rubber, I won the second. I know he will win the finals, for the cards are stacked: he has all the aces. But when?" [12] Ornifle will continue to enjoy his immorality until all of the cards are dealt and God decides to reveal his winning hand.

The moral laxity of Ornifle is complemented by the unscrupulousness of Machetu, his boorish public relations manager. Machetu, having had a youth of poverty, has now become extraordinarily wealthy by selling Ornifle's rhymes. He is the most antipathetic of characters: he is distrustful, constantly on his guard against friend and foe, and is completely devoid of sentiment, for Mammon has replaced the soul he had when he was poor. Machetu is the epitome of society's abuses, its underhanded practices, its prostitution of art, its venality.

This laxity on the part of Ornifle and Machetu is contrasted with Fabrice's rigorous abstention from wine and women, and his determination to avenge his mother (who had been seduced by Ornifle). He always carries on his person the weapon with which he will avenge her; he symbolizes the intransigent hero who is ever victimized by society. Fabrice had vowed to his mother that medicine would be an apostolate for him, and his life since her death has been continuous suffering and deprivation, with enforced simplicity of desires and stoicism. Fabrice is pure and ingenuous, and genuinely in love with Marguerite.

Symbolically, it is Fabrice who holds Ornifle's life in his hands: Fabrice's pistol threatens his father, Fabrice's diagnosis of Ornifle's heart disease dooms him. Neither Machetu's raking in of millions for Ornifle nor the fortune spent by Ornifle to keep his precious body under the constant surveillance of two medical specialists can save the hedonist from the death reserved for him in the form of the humble Fabrice, who provides—as is indicated by the subtitle of the play—a simple draft of fresh air.

CHAPTER 7

Pièces costumées

THE *pièces costumées,* together with *Pauvre Bitos* (1956), the last of the "jarring" plays, make up the list of historical plays written by Anouilh. *L'Alouette* (1953) tells the story of Joan of Arc; *Becket* (1959) relates the tragic friendship between Henry Plantagenet and Becket; *La Foire d'empoigne* (1962) deals with Napoleon and Louis XVIII.

The plays having as their central characters mythological and legendary heroes—*Eurydice* (1941), *Antigone* (1942), *Oreste* (1945), *Médée* (1946)—will also be treated here, for historical and mythological figures share common elements of mysteriousness, permanency, and immutability. In his plays based upon myth, Anouilh purposefully employed the original plots, reinterpreting them (as had André Gide, Jean Cocteau, and Jean Giraudoux before him) in accordance with a general post-World War I movement away from realism and toward stylization, fantasy, and symbolism.

What Anouilh has said about Joan of Arc applies to all of the characters in the *pièces costumées:* "You cannot explain Joan any more than you can explain the tiniest flower growing by the wayside. There it is—just a little living flower that has always known, ever since it was a microscopic seed, how many petals it would have and how big they would grow, exactly how blue its blue would be and how its delicate scent would be compounded." [1]

Jason predicts that there will never be other Medeas on this earth, that mothers will never name their daughters Medea, and that the Medea he knows at the very moment he addresses her will stand alone until the end of time. At the close of the play, as she and her children are being devoured by flames, she will proclaim: "I am Medea, finally and forever." [2] Nevertheless, Medea has become almost a stock character in Anouilh's plays: she is the young woman of the lesser race who carries her head high, clenches her fists, scornfully spits upon the ground and stamps her feet in defiance. She survives through the ages: Antigone, Joan of Arc, "la sauvage," Jeannette, Adèle (of La Grotte)—they are all atavisms of Medea.

History, for Anouilh, is a continuous and confused play: reigns are intermissions, as kings appear on thrones and reappear from exile, changing the number suffixed to their name as they come and go. Louis XVIII in La Foire d'empoigne, referring to his very old countenance, not even of his own making,[3] speaks of the countenance shared by all kings, the common denominator in their uninterrupted role.

Historic figures make revolutions with their words; they are actors and all the world's their stage. History is a "foire d'empoigne" —a "game of grab." Kings snatch from emperors, Popes from kings, the people from nobles and vice versa. Napoleon's final bit of advice to his loyal and devoted lieutenant is not to despair at the fall of the Empire, but rather to don a mask and costume and join in the game of grab, either by assassinating the king, or by becoming a revolutionary Carbonaro or a radical Jacobin.

Anouilh suggests that the soul and the personality of man remain unchanged: it is the mask and the costume that vary to suit a given era, to divert and provoke the tears and laughter of each generation. Although the playwright sees political situations as patently ridiculous, his mournful political characters treat them with sober and virtuous solemnity; for Anouilh, the melancholy spectacle of world problems, poverty, and war is being played out by laughing but brokenhearted clowns.

The General in L'Hurluberlu had told his son: "You'll find out, as you get older, that even when life seems to be serious, it's nothing but a Punch and Judy show. And that we're always giving the same play over and over."[4] History is a farce, in true commedia dell'arte style. Government is merely the art of duping people into believing that they themselves think, while it is actually those in power who control thought. History's games are indeed the same throughout the centuries; Robespierre's frenzied revolutionary measures are not different from uprisings of this and future centuries.

Most of the plays in the "costumed" category are presented as improvisations, with characters fitting into their historical roles on stage, mixing reality with illusion, and changing the sequence and accuracy of history for the desired dramatic effects. In *Médée* the heroine directs the assignment of roles to play out the horrendous tragedy. She tells her Nurse not to interfere with the unfolding of the drama of destruction: "The game we are playing is not for you." [5] On the other hand, to the bearer of the news of Jason's impending marriage to Creusa, which dissolves the self-destructive union between Jason and Medea and allows the heroine to give vent to her hatred, she offers encouragement to speak: "Hurry, hurry, little one, and you will finish your role, you'll be able to go back and enjoy yourself." [6] Jason, too, feels that he must play out his role eternally: "I can prevent nothing from happening. I can just about play the role assigned to me, forever." [7]

I   Antigone

For his adaptation of the Antigone story Anouilh retains the basic outlines of Aeschylus' and Sophocles' versions, but introduces several anachronisms—breakfasts of coffee and buttered tartines, racing cars and nightclubs, guards armed with automatic rifles—which help to emphasize certain truths that do not change with time. In his *Le Songe du critique* Anouilh had defended the use of modern dress in *Tartuffe* by maintaining that the Molière play is a "bourgeois story," and that therefore it is reasonable to clothe the characters in the costume of our uncles and grandmothers. Likewise in *Antigone,* since the play is a study of revolt against a bourgeois order, the modern dress of the characters is justified.

The setting for *Antigone* is Thebes. When the curtain rises all of the play's characters are seated on the stage. The Prologue steps forward and tells the audience that King Oedipus, who blinded himself and was banished from Thebes after killing his father and then marrying his mother, has died. The throne had been given to his two sons, Eteocles and Polynices, who were to alternate as rulers one year at a time. After the first-year reign Eteocles, the older son, had refused to yield his power to his brother, as had been predetermined, and a civil war ensued during which the two brothers killed each other. Creon, brother of Oedipus' mother Jocasta, took over the duties as king.

Since Creon had sided with Eteocles for political reasons, he decreed that Eteocles be given burial rites, but that Polynices' body be left unburied to be eaten by vultures. Death would be the penalty for anyone who attempted to mourn or bury him. Now, only the daughters of Oedipus remain: Antigone and Ismene. Creon's son, Haemon, is in love with Antigone and the two are to be married.

At this point the immobile characters on the stage stir, and the play begins. Antigone, having disregarded her uncle's edict, has buried her brother. She is caught and confesses willingly. Antigone debates with Creon the question of the supremacy of divine law, which demands the burial of the dead, over human law, including the law of kings. She is put into a cave to die and moments later hangs herself. As the cave is being sealed off Creon hears the moans of his son from within. He calls out to him, but Haemon takes the dead Antigone into his arms and then stabs himself. Creon's wife Eurydice, unable to bear the tragedy of her son's death, cuts her throat. Creon is left to carry on his kingly duties alone.

With the death of Antigone, life in Thebes returns to normal (as is usual in classical tragedy). The king goes off to his council meeting and the guards continue to play cards. Without Antigone, life again becomes flat and colorless. Hypocrites and compromisers can play their roles undisturbed. "And there it is," the Chorus tells us at the end of the play. "Without little Antigone, it's true, they all might have been peaceful." [8]

Although both Antigone and Creon are intransigent figures, each convinced that his view is the only one, the clash is more than the opposition of a realist and an idealist. Antigone's protest against established order and Creon's collaboration with values of compromise are equally without hope of creating something better. Neither Antigone nor Creon suggests reform or change, and, in the end, neither of the two argues his views logically. Each derives a certain pleasure and fulfillment from the mere assertion of his will.

There is no communication between the king and his niece. Creon's temperament, so opposed to Antigone's, does not allow him at first to understand her, especially after he reveals how unworthy Polynices was of her concern. For a short time Antigone, crushed by Creon's logical arguments, sits passively. Then Creon makes his fatal error: he tells Antigone to marry and find her happiness with Haemon. This formula automatically antagonizes the Anouilh heroine. The picture of the *petit bonheur* of the masses as a life of compromise and mediocrity, contrary to her demands for a perpetual state of happiness, shocks Antigone into reasserting her defiance. She thereupon taunts her uncle until he is forced to call the guards. Only then does Creon understand her revolt. Polynices was merely a pretext; Antigone's *raison d'être* is to be put to death.

While many of Anouilh's other heroines are adults seeking to purge themselves of their miserable past, Antigone is the eternally innocent child with a rebellious temperament and a preference for solitude. When Creon crushes the sense of moral obligation that might have justified her burying Polynices, she admits that her persistence is "for no one. For myself." [9] What began as a moral issue becomes the strongest affirmation of personal revolt. Of necessity, the burial of Polynices must not be considered a moral choice, for Antigone is caught in the workings of an infernal machine and there are no alternatives for her. She is a puppet playing a preordained part; her choice is fatal, not free.

Antigone's violation of the law is committed solely to satisfy the internal exigencies of her character which demand an abstract "no" in defiance of all of the Creons in this world and ultimately in defiance of life itself. Her dignity lies in the absolute negation of life, in the automatic refusal and rejection of all bourgeois standards.

It is not difficult for Antigone to renounce even Haemon, because the idea that he will grow older and make compromises, as had his father, is unbearable: "I love a young and hard Haemon, a Haemon demanding and faithful, like me. . . . But if the wear and tear of your life, your happiness, must change him in any way . . . then I no longer love Haemon." [10] Antigone is reminiscent of Ibsen's uncompromising Brand, for whom "the enemy" is personified as the spirit of compromise, the spirit of the *juste milieu*. Death, then, becomes a refuge and a deliverance from this damnable existence.

II Oreste

Like *Antigone, Oreste* opens with all of the characters on stage. Aegisthus steps forward to announce that the dramatis personae are going to play a game teaming Electra and Orestes against Aegisthus and Clytemnestra. The game will consist of untiringly throwing a red ball among the four players. The ball will burn their hands and the earth will be covered with blood; the score will be kept eternally in letters as large as man, on a scoreboard behind the players. Electra then steps forward to identify herself. She screams out her name. Aegisthus explains that the reason she screams is that she is still young and does not yet know how to play the game well. Her role is to incite her brother to avenge the murder of their father, Agamemnon, and to keep the memory of that murder vivid in Aegisthus' mind.

A silent Orestes is described as "a little black, burned monkey, with eyes that are too big, and who never wanted to talk" [11]; he had seen his mother Clytemnestra making love to Aegisthus, after which he never again smiled, for he had learned too much at the age of four. Aegisthus explains that, after the murder of Orestes' father by Clytemnestra, Orestes was taken up to the mountains to be raised by an old hermit. Aegisthus did not send his men to kill the boy, for he sensed that Orestes *had* to live, had to grow up and take his vengeance (by slaying Aegisthus and Clytemnestra). Neither did Aegisthus cause Electra to be killed; he assumed that she was harmless, that she could be treated as a servant, married off to a peasant boy and tied down to immobility by twelve children.

Instead, Electra pursues her vengeance by becoming a child of hate and destruction. She purposely renders herself ugly and dirty, rips her dresses, and rubs her skin against the lepers huddled at the walls of the palace of Argos. She has taken all mirrors from her room because she knows and fears the self-created monster of destruction that will call Aegisthus and Clytemnestra out of the palace to die.

Although Electra is frightened and cries out her lines on stage, Aegisthus, on the night that he knows he is going to die, feels calm, rested, rejuvenated, and without bitterness; he is finally able to sleep the sleep of a child who has just been pardoned. His death will be his liberation from the memory of his crime, which has been resounding implacably in his ears from the moment of its commission.

Although Anouilh published only fragments of *Oreste,* the fragments are sufficient to reveal the concepts of the "costumed" play and of the "savage" hero and heroine. All the characters are aware that they are playing a game—a death game—and that it must be played out to the end. The intransigent race of Orestes and Elec-

tra views its elders' crimes as unpardonable and its own vengeance as ineluctable. The ineffaceable image of their father's
death obsesses Orestes and Electra and renders them *sauvages*.
Electra constantly reminds her brother that their father was killed
in his armor; that, when he fell, throughout the palace was heard
the "sinister noise of saucepans"—the anachronistic element in the
eloquent description of Agamemnon dying with his boots on. To
remind Aegisthus of his crime, Electra steals into the kitchen late
at night to throw pots and pans down onto the stone floor. Each
time, Aegisthus did hear Electra's message in "that triumphant
clatter on the flagstones." [12]

Electra sees as the worst aspect of the crime the fact that her
very tall father, in his armor, fell full-length onto the ground:
"You understand, Orestes . . . they not only killed our father,
they made him fall straight out on the ground." [13] It is that image
which constitutes the absurdity of Electra's intransigence. It is
comparable to Antigone's insistence not so much on avenging her
brother as on the necessity of carrying out the burial rites for
someone she is not even sure is Polynices. Destiny demands that
their somewhat absurd concept of duty be played out to its tragic
end.

III   Eurydice *and* Médée

This same fatalism also pervades the two "black" plays based
upon legend, *Eurydice* and *Médée*. In Anouilh's adaptation of the
Orpheus legend Eurydice would like to purify herself of her past
love affairs by marrying Orpheus, but she is too weak to make the
symbolic confession to her lover. In despair, she runs away and
dies in a bus accident. A mysterious Monsieur Henri tells the dis-
consolate Orpheus that Eurydice will be returned to him, provid-
ing that he does not look into her eyes (symbolic of looking into
her past) before an established time. Orpheus, tormented by his
jealousy and his passion for truth, cannot refrain from looking at
his beloved, and thus loses her again. The lovers are eventually
united in the eternal afterlife, death being the only realm in which
the past cannot destroy happiness.

As in *Antigone*, the characters of the legend are put into a modern setting and reenact their tragedy in circumstances quite different from those of mythology. The hero and heroine are of the
"poor race," with the heavy baggage of their past corruption on

their backs. They are embarrassed by their poverty and by the vulgarity and niggardliness of their parents. After falling instantly in love, Orpheus and Eurydice exchange magical words that make them realize that they are *petits frères* without even knowing each other's name. They find momentary happiness in their vision of a "pure" love, but by the end of Act I, which serves as a prologue, the hero begins questioning the heroine about her past, which she tries to cover, exactly as does Jeannette in *Roméo et Jeannette.* As the curtain falls on the first act, Orpheus says "the story is now beginning," and each asks the name of the other.

A night spent together in a sordid provincial hotel room serves to intensify Eurydice's horror of her past, even though her love for Orpheus fills her with strength and courage to face the world. She is obsessed with her inability to be sincere; her past is stuck to her skin and confessing it does not cleanse her of it—rather, the repetition of stories of ugly persons of her past who live within her may fortify their existence.

After Eurydice's death, Orpheus, who has not been able to discern the truth about her, is inconsolable. Although in this case Monsieur Henri makes an exception to the law of death, Orpheus is obsessed with his solitude. He sees each human being living in his own skin, with his own blood and his own organs. He would like to be drowned completely in Eurydice's blood and intertwine his organs with hers, but to do this he must know the truth about her. In defiance of Monsieur Henri's admonitions not to look at the "dead" Eurydice until dawn, Orpheus turns around to question his beloved. The spell is broken. All of the characters of Eurydice's sordid past invade the stage. She blushes with shame, announcing that now she will leave the earth forever.

Eurydice then fades away, as do all of the other characters except Orpheus and his father, who crushes his son with banal talk about trains, menus, and appreciation of the fact that his son has not abandoned him. Monsieur Henri reappears to tell Orpheus that life is like an old jacket waiting to be put on each morning. Orpheus retorts that he will not put his on this morning, to which Monsieur Henri asks whether Orpheus has a substitute. Orpheus, unlike Gaston in *Le Voyageur sans bagage,* does not have another jacket to slip into, for his belief that his love for Eurydice could have been eternal and different from other loves has been torn into shreds by Monsieur Henri.

Only Orpheus' death will allow him to hold eternally the original young and pure Eurydice; his death will permit her to be eternally "herself." The play closes with the reenactment of the previous act in which Monsieur Henri had permitted the lovers to be reunited, but this time Orpheus may look at Eurydice; through death they may merge into one new person, free from the contingencies of life and morality. Their "black" legend lasts, and is relived in each generation's game of death.

IV   L'Alouette

L'Alouette is Anouilh's version of the Joan of Arc story. All of the main characters in Joan's life appear simultaneously on the stage at the start of the play. The opening lines are Warwick's, expressing his haste to see Joan judged and burned. Cauchon protests that the whole story must be played out, and, throughout the drama, he stresses the fact that each character is playing his role, as it is written, whether it be good or bad, each in his turn.

Joan is being diverted from the task that God has assigned her by her parents, her king, the Church, and the enemies of France. Joan's mother, Baudricourt, King Charles, the Inquisitor, and Warwick attempt to save her but she is well aware that she has taken the first step toward her doom and that no one can dissuade her from undergoing her auto-da-fé. Joan turns a deaf ear to those who live and change with the times, for her truth is not relative but absolute. If the hours destined for her to live will not run counterclockwise, she will at least have demonstrated the eternal truth of her cause, which is to be true to herself and her God. Cauchon, the Bishop of Beauvais, in whose besieged diocese Joan had been captured by the English, is a tragic figure. He knows what honor required of him, yet is too mediocre to make the supreme sacrifice that might have prevented the surrender of Joan to the English.

Joan's honor demands that she save France from the English and thereby serve God. What a mockery, then, are her father's protests: "Save France? Save France? And, in the meanwhile, who will take care of my cows?" [14] What a mockery of the Church are the words of the Inquisition's representative describing the beautiful forms the devil assumes in order to tempt man. With

devastating simplicity, Joan defends God's honor by retorting that
"the devil is ugly and everything beautiful is the work of God." [15]

Anouilh's Joan of Arc is a Christian Antigone whose legend is
reduced to the dimensions of a simple human adventure, with elements of grotesqueness and buffoonery. Joan has the same stub-
born pride as Antigone; she accepts it as a gift from God. Joan,
like Antigone, is aware of her solitude and faces her destiny alone.
Even the voices which set her on her path of adventure are silent
as she stands before her executioners. Like Antigone and Becket,
she will be faithful to the concept of honor which she has conceived for herself, yet she cannot help deploring the heavy weight
of the burden.

Joan confesses to her father, in words evocative of Antigone's to
her Nurse: "I am so alone, so small, and it's so heavy. . . . I'm so
tired of struggling all alone." [16] Joan and Antigone are revolting
against an established secular or religious order—referred to as
the *Idea* in *L'Alouette*—that serves as a fascistic safeguard in
dealing with the mediocre race. They affirm their ideal against the
base compromises that the State or the Church demands in the
name of duty and obedience.

Joan's words are the standard refusal of the "insolent breed":
"All you can do is kill me, make me cry out anything under tor-
ture, but you can't make me say 'yes'!" [17] The refusal of Joan of Arc
to recant is a victory for truth—the truth of a pure, naïve, humble,
and sensitive young girl who defies the reasoning of theologians.
Joan needs neither the Church nor the Inquisition to reveal God's
truth to her; her childlike ingenuousness senses instinctively that
everything beautiful is God's creation, and she does not need the
village curé to inform her when the devil is present.

The trial of Joan for heresy is intended to demonstrate the heroism of the individual who holds his head high to defend the greatness of man even when God seems to have abandoned him.
Against the Inquisitor, whose fanaticism leads him to destroy sin-
ful humanity, Joan defends the dignity of the "pure" being who
does both good and evil specifically because God created him for
this contradiction. Joan's world is peopled with "savages," yet she
knows that it is the Kingdom of Heaven.

V   Becket

Becket, ou l'Honneur de Dieu, written six years after *L'Alou-ette,* is in many ways similar to the earlier play. In *Becket,* Anouilh presents the conflict between two men who dearly love each other but who become antagonists. Becket, the Saxon, who at one time strongly defended the interest and honor of the Norman king of England against the Church, eventually finds himself, as archbishop of Canterbury, defending the honor of God and the Church against the abuse of the king.

Like Joan of Arc, Thomas à Becket accepts his transformation from bosom companion to Henry II into the role for which he had been eternally destined; he is now the archbishop, and must champion a divine order against the temporal order of the kingdom. Like Joan, he will play out his assigned role without even attempting to convert his adversary to his point of view: "I don't have to convince you. All I have to do is say 'no' to you." [18] Both Joan and Becket have resigned themselves to their somewhat absurd fate and make no effort to revolt against it.

The curtain rises on the crypt of Canterbury cathedral, where Henry II, kneeling at the tomb of Becket, awaits public chastisement and discovers how painful the memory of love and friendship can be. As the king examines his conscience, the drama of friendship unfolds. The confidence, admiration, fidelity, and love between the young Saxon and the king are reenacted. As long as Becket hunted, took counsel concerning ways to diminish the exorbitant power of the clergy in England, and shared refinements and pleasures with his royal friend, no conflict between God and king arose. As soon as Henry places Becket upon the episcopal throne, however, the concept of defending God's honor against the king's honor takes shape in Becket's mind. The cruel rupture between the two friends is intensified by the love that they still feel for each other. Nevertheless, the archbishop of Canterbury's role henceforth will be to take an irreconcilable position against Henry in a *dialogue de sourds.*

Exiled in France, Becket meets with Henry on an icy plain. For a few moments their love prompts them desperately to want to help each other, to search for a formula that will allow the honor of God to coincide with the honor of the king in an ordered world in which Becket will be able to see his king as his true prince. Henry and Becket soon realize, however, that they will grow old and cold before this aspiration is realized. Each returns to England on his own, where their implacable conflict will continue until Becket falls under the swords of the English barons.

The close of the play is the enactment of Henry's public penitence: the monks come into the crypt, remove the crown from the king's head, strip him to the waist and scourge him. Henry cries out: "Are you satisfied, Becket? Has the honor of God been met in full?" [19]

Anouilh conceived the structure of the play as the diametrical opposition between the corpulent, jovial, sensual king, whose personality is clearly defined, and the double-personality Saxon, who is more ambiguous. The latter pursues his frivolous pleasures cynically yet elegantly, and he searches for his place in life somewhere between the king's side and the outstretched arms of the masses of the poor; nowhere does he find intellectual challenges, for the learned clerics of Becket's Church and the intemperate noblemen of his palace are equidistant from true knowledge. As a Saxon, Becket belongs to an oppressed minority that had been crushed by the Norman conquerors. Although he has become the bosom companion of King Henry, he can never forget that history's wheels have been turned by dying Saxons, and he senses that, in the future, the wheels will be lubricated by dying Normans. He tells Henry: "If you were of my race, how simple everything would be." [20]

Henry and Becket are of separate races, yet the cares and problems of the oppressed race have lain dormant long enough for the love-friendship relationship to develop between the two men. If Henry's love may be characterized as idealistic, Becket's is realistic, lucid, and without illusion. Henry could not sense that by naming Becket archbishop of Canterbury their love might be destroyed. Becket, on the other hand, knows that life is a role to be played, and that, in order to live, he must play the part assigned to him, even at the sacrifice of love.

Becket's defense of the honor of God is somewhat different from Joan of Arc's: Joan remains humble and God-fearing throughout her drama, while Becket seems to be afraid of no one, not even God. He has a profound belief in his own judgments and

values, and thinks that he stands above the vain distinctions between good and evil—distinctions useful for the masses and for
the necessities of social order. He is flippant about the Absolute,
and the Little Monk (his *alter ego* in the play) mocks Becket's
prayers. His religious belief in God is questionable, yet the beauty
of his mistress, Gwendolyn, is for him "one of those rare things
that confirm the existence of God." [21]

Since the kingdom of God is defended with the same brutality
as earthly kingdoms, Becket has no hope that religion will temper
human history. It is a realistic Becket who performs his duty esthetically, not because God's voice has inspired him but because
his principle of morality is to do what has to be done, when it has
to be done, and to do it well. A simple human convention rather
than a divine commandment is the *deus ex machina* of Becket's
drama.

As archbishop, Becket very logically adopts the only attitude
conducive to the playing out of his own concept of honor: every
gesture, every action, must be the beautiful, elegant, and perfect
expression of an archbishop's defense of the honor of God. The
former dandy will dismiss his concubines, give away his gold and
his sables, dress in a rough serge robe and oppose the beloved
king who opposes the power of the primatial archbishop. Becket
the dilettante thus finds a mooring to which he can attach a
weighty concept of honor.

Having rejected a facile and improvised way of life in favor of
this burdensome honor, Becket's existence is now meaningful, and
the world around him will become ordered. He has fortuitously
been offered an absolute truth that he will serve loyally until his
death: God's—or Becket's—honor. Is he a saint or a fool? A traitor
or a wanderer who finally finds his way? The answers to these
questions depend upon each individual's view of what constitutes
the honor of man.

VI   La Foire d'empoigne

La Foire d'empoigne presents us with Anouilh's version of
Napoleon as a soulless opportunist who bases his every move
upon the impression it will create. The emperor politely awaits
the exit of Louis XVIII before returning for one hundred days to
give a noble ending to his melodrama. Louis XVIII, charming,
practical, and realistic, plays history's game of grab, bargaining

for his supporters and snatching anything worthwhile left behind by Napoleon.

Fouché, servant of two masters, shuttles obsequiously between king and emperor, and states that he is "making history," illustrating perfectly the Anouilh theme of the relativity of time. The final monologue of Napoleon, now prisoner of the English, is quite different from the classical tragic style anticipated by Fouché, and is touched with wry humor and cynicism, as d'Anouville, the emperor's chief admirer, loses his youthful idealism.

Again, Anouilh has brought to the stage in *La Foire d'empoigne* historical figures who recognize that they are actors playing roles in the drama that is French history. In this play there are no heroes, no ennobling concepts, and no defenders of honor. Only a very ridiculous duke stands ready to make a rampart of his thin body to protect his corpulent king against assassins. An irresolute idealist, whose only ambition is to die for his emperor, subsequently decides to compromise, as the king suggested he should.

Napoleon is inglorious and unheroic: he has historical jitters, which he tries to calm by associating with a gallery of rogues, because he knows that his marshals are ready to desert him if the king offers them more money. The success of his domestic policy lies in bribing churchmen, for "he who controls the curé controls the woman, and who controls the woman controls the man." [22]

Louis XVIII is equally inglorious: to the horror of his faithful followers who have emigrated and remained with him during his nineteen years of exile, he haggles over the prices offered by his would-be allies. When the idealistic Lieutenant d'Anouville attempts to assassinate him, King Louis grants him pardon (which is temporarily refused in a scene reminiscent of *Antigone*), but he taunts the "glorious hero" concept and insinuates that d'Anouville would do better to accept *le petit bonheur*.

The king's words destroy the fragile makings of a hero in the person of d'Anouville. As Napoleon, being taken away by the English, shouts to him to cover himself with glory, the young lieutenant disillusions the emperor by responding that he will marry and have children. The curtain falls as Napoleon warns d'Anouville not to teach those children too much about ideals, for "they do not constitute life's luggage." [23]

Thus, *La Foire d'empoigne* ends in compromise and mediocrity. Idealism, honor, devotion, and duty to one's country, king and/or emperor are meaningless. The heroism of an Antigone, a Joan of Arc, or a Becket, is nipped in the bud by a sordid assortment of history's so-called "greats."

VII   Pauvre Bitos

Belief in one's own power is one of the oldest comic situations in history. The solemn and well-meaning character who thinks that he can do everything but stumbles into the depths of ridiculousness is embodied in Anouilh's version of Robespierre in *Pauvre Bitos, ou le Dîner de têtes*. The subtitle, besides evoking heads severed by the guillotine during the French Revolution, reveals that *Pauvre Bitos* is a play being played, for a *dîner de têtes* is a wig party at which the guests wear the disguise of historic personages.

Maxime, the director of the play within the play, has asked a group of friends to study the figures of the French Revolution. He will invite them to his home for a sinister *dîner de têtes*. The dinner will serve as a farewell to his mansion, which is about to be converted into a gasoline station because Maxime no longer wishes to be reminded of his aristocratic ancestors who politely allowed themselves to be guillotined instead of defending themselves as men. The wig party is also an excuse for Maxime to coerce André Bitos into assuming the identity of the fanatical Robespierre. Bitos is a merciless and unyielding deputy public prosecutor who has returned to the town of his birth to mete out cold and cruel justice and to fill the region with sentiments of Jacobinism, rigor, and virtue.

Maxime and his aristocratic friends detest Bitos, partly because he is of poor and second-rate origin, partly because he was always the best student in the class. The wig party will be an opportunity for them to taunt, mock, scorn, shame, and humiliate him, and finally threaten his life, under the cover of their disguises and their historically-based arguments. Maxime is delighted that Victoire, the attractive daughter of the President of the Tribunal who has refused her hand to Bitos, has accepted his invitation. Her presence will serve as an excuse for stressing Bitos' physical inferiority and gracelessness and his ridiculous fear of women.

Each guest, in modern dress but wearing a wig of the French Revolutionary period, represents and must enact in speech and behavior a revolutionary figure: Saint Just, Danton, Marie Antoinette, Tallien and his wife, Camille and Lucille Desmoulins, and Mirabeau. Bitos, virtually kidnaped, arrives, and the attack begins. The guests lash out not only at Robespierre and the Revolution, but simultaneously at Bitos, who represents the provincial leftist Resistance leaders who were still wreaking vengeance upon the detested wealthy collaborators ten years after the close of World War II.

The combination of the guests' ruthlessness, wine, and a feigned pistol shot succeeds in rendering the abstemious Bitos senseless. In his unconscious state, he finds himself obliged to defend simultaneously three aspects of himself—a studious schoolboy, a public prosecutor, and a terrorist—and he is unsure who he really is. He recalls his own past life, but it is so embroiled with incidents of Robespierre's life that now Bitos is clearly an avatar of his murderously vindictive antecedent.

At the end of the play the half-recovered Bitos is invited by his host to bury their differences in a few drinks at a night club. Victoire warns Bitos not to accept Maxime's false gesture of friendship, for she knows that Maxime intends only to humiliate him further. She reveals that, even though her father refused Bitos's marriage offer and even though she could never love him, still she will always love his poverty and admire his courage and rigor. Humbly, she tells him to guard his poverty carefully, and never to forget his coat of arms—the rough, reddened arms of his mother, a laundress. Bitos thanks Victoire for her warning, but his last words are that if ever he is able to avenge himself for the *dîner de têtes* he will begin with her—the only one who has shown him a bit of kindness. She sighs "Pauvre Bitos!" as the curtain falls.

The character of Bitos-Robespierre is a doubly intense personification of hatred. Bitos' hatred stems from the inferiority complex that has been instilled in him by the "rich race"; Robespierre's is the historical manifestation of man's externalization of his insufficiencies and inner feelings. André Bitos, as a child, was constantly reminded by his vicious schoolmates that he was nothing but the graceless son of a poverty-stricken laundress. His response was to drive himself ruthlessly in order to excel as a student, which further antagonized his peers and led the Jesuits to accuse him of pride and vanity. He was cruelly chastised for his lack of flexibility, but always refused to ask forgiveness in order to avoid the strokes of the Jesuits' rods. Bitos is reminiscent of Medea who, when asked by Creon to leave Corinth without seeing Jason again, replied: "I cannot beg you. My knees cannot bend, my voice cannot grow humble." [24]

As a man, Bitos is the leftist version of the General in *L'Hurlu-berlu:* his concept of honor and duty is inhuman. He will set the example of "purity" for all men, and for those who do not fit into his totalitarian machine he will cause "horrible suffering" for the good of the nation. His obsession with punishing men derives partly from fear of the masses and partly from a personal desire for revenge. Bitos-Robespierre rebukes Mirabeau for his volatility and urges him to forget youth and gaiety in order to help "clean" France.

No one has ever seen Bitos asleep. He has never been loved by a woman, nor has he ever shared erotic thoughts with men. He knows that he will never be able to please anyone, so he sets himself apart in a tower of rigor and relentless law. Unflinchingly he will send his dearest friend to the guillotine; killing is his implement for fashioning order, which he loves more than men. Only on his deathbed does Robespierre finally realize the futility of the Revolution: "All this noise, all these gestures, this fury, this agitation, this hatred and these wounds, are that and nothing else; and now everything is falling into order . . . in death. . . . But it took a long time to find out." [25]

Men do not learn from history's mistakes, nor does Bitos learn from his incarnation as Robespierre. *Pauvre Bitos* is a gripping and bitter indictment of Frenchmen of all times and of all political persuasions. Anouilh is as ruthless with the masses as with the aristocracy, historical and present. No one is spared. Never has the playwright exposed all of mankind with such caustic candor nor with such thoroughness.

CHAPTER 8

Anouilh's Dramatic Technique

I The Dramatist's Task

ANOUILH once declared that his conception of the dramatist's task is above all to respond to the actors' need for plays
that will divert the public from its worries and thoughts of death,
and only incidentally to create from time to time a masterpiece.[1]
The first obligation of the dramatist, then, is to the actors, and the
second to the audience; active complicity on the part of both actor
and audience is necessary, so that the play becomes a natural conversation between them. Madame de Montalembreuse in *Le Rendez-vous de Senlis* describes this essential relationship in a meta-
phor of a wild, rearing horse (the spectators) that has to be
broken in by a tamer (the actor) who feels the emotions of the
horse, and vibrates and harmonizes with it.[2]

Anouilh's ideal of the unity of players and spectators is expressed in *La Répétition* by the Count, who insists that the Marivaux play being rehearsed in his château begin at the dinner
table. The characters will rise to speak to one another, with the
butler joining in, while the other guests (the audience) will remain seated. The play will thus begin smoothly, without the
dreaded "curtain going up" moment, and without any chance of
stopping the natural and physiological process of a presentation
whose dramatic necessities have been elicited, as it were, from the
dinner menu. The play should come from the very bowels of the
actors and the audience.

In the Marivaux play, Sylvia and Harlequin love each other
dearly. The natural flow of words between them in the "rehearsal"
is duplicated in the "real" words of the Count and Lucile, for
whom a true harmony exists because they, too, are in love. Similarly, a natural attachment must bind actors and spectators in
order to yield a spectacle that will be "truer than true"—that is,
the spectacle of Harlequin's beautiful world of improvisation and
illusion, where everyone can escape from the menace of poverty

and politics, where endless surprises are made and unmade, where masks of tragedy and comedy can be changed at a moment's notice, and where love ultimately reigns supreme. By playing on his marionettes' emotional strings, in harmony with audience reactions, the playwright is best able to create a fanciful world of illusion into which the public can escape from the pressures of the real world.

John Harvey has written: "The meaning of [Anouilh's] theatre lies in its nature as 'play,' the simple game of pretending. Most of us have grown up to be spectators in the game and we need interpreters to maintain the make-believe before us, and dramatists to supply the matter for our uninventive minds. We must be willful accomplices to the game, accepting its rules and conventions, freely tasting of it with intellect and feeling." [3]

II Commedia dell'arte *Techniques*

Audience complicity was, of course, the keystone of the old *commedia dell'arte*, the theatrical tradition into which Anouilh has deliberately sought to fit his plays, applying the "playing" technique to drama as well as comedy. The reader will recall that the eternal stock characters of the old Italian comedy appeared with different disguises and different personalities for the various scenarios: Harlequin, sometimes jovial and sometimes pathetic, portrayed the knave, the trickster, the silly woman, and the ridiculous bourgeois. Pulcinella with his two humps, one in front, one behind, was the combination of two ancient Roman stock characters: Maccus, who was lively, witty, insolent, and a little ferocious, and Bucco, who was a self-satisfied flatterer, a boaster, a thief, and a coward. Pulcinella upheld both sides in the battle of the sexes; he understood both the young and the old; what belonged to others belonged to him; he feared neither God nor the devil, for he could always escape to his *alter ego*. Spavento, the daring captain in a three-cornered hat which, to the bewilderment of his audience, turned in the directions of three simultaneous duels, was the *commedia dell'arte*'s active hero, attached to no one, shying from no challenge, and symbolic of mobility. Pantalon was portrayed sometimes as a garrulous, mean, miserly old man, sometimes as a silly, tottering dotard in his spectacles and slippers; in one play he inspired laughter, in the next, pity.

The world of the *commedia dell'arte* characters was one of fantasy, a mixture of the grotesque and the ideal. Accordingly, the characters were figures to whom psychological consistency was denied: they were one, no one, and a hundred thousand others. The purpose of the *commedia* spectacles, of the complicated intrigues that made light of reality and juggled with incoherences, was to help the audience escape and deny the value of reality.

The scenarios were simply outlines of plots, with indications as to which characters were to appear and under what circumstances, without any written dialogue provided. The improvised plot was "rehearsed" for a few hours before the performance by actors who had a store of previously memorized "repertory," under the guidance of a director who set the place and scene of the action and the exact relation of the characters to one another. Singers and ballet dancers provided variety and movement, and basic stage tricks added the final touches to a complete *commedia dell'arte* spectacle.

Stylization and improvisation thus characterized the *commedia dell'arte*. Anouilh's plays are stylized to the extent that a conflict between illusion and reality, between an ideal and a compromise, is artificially constructed. At the same time, however, there is room for enough improvisation to satisfy the needs of a particular troupe or a particular audience. A footnote to Act IV of *La Répétition* reveals Anouilh's appreciation of improvised techniques: he invites considerable shearing or complete cutting of this longish act by directors and actors who may find it to be out of keeping with the rest of the play. Anouilh, the technician, "plays" with his characters. He feels that his dramas can be improvised, remade constantly, changed and rechanged. His theater, like the old Italian comedy, is not static, even though fixed character types appear and reappear in the plays.

The troupes that presented the improvised *commedias* became identified with their particular theater and featured no principal actor or actress—each player performed in many roles, indiscriminately, and only the mask remained unchanged. Thus, the problem of tailoring roles to individual actors was in those days nonexistent. Today, however, this is not the case, and Anouilh dramatizes his grappling with this problem in several of his plays. In *Le Rendez-vous de Senlis* the fifty-two-year-old actor, who sees himself as a dashing young lover, is grievously insulted because the "director" insists that he should play the father role without makeup. Likewise, his feminine counterpart protests that she is a prima donna—not a mother. In *La Répétition* and in *La Grotte* Anouilh's spokesmen describe how difficult it is to deal with actors who assume that the play is over as soon as they have spoken their lines.

On the other hand, one of Anouilh's ideal *commedia* types is his eternal, unchangeable, stock butler who, in *La Grotte*, reminisces about his unending utility to the Author (Anouilh himself): "I have served Monsieur well: *Le Voyageur sans bagage*, 1937; *Léocadia*, 1940; *Le Rendez-vous de Senlis*, 1941; *L'Invitation au Château*, 1947; Monsieur has always been very satisfied with my services. Monsieur even loaned me once to Oscar Wilde, for an adaptation on which Monsieur collaborated." [4]

It is in this same play, *La Grotte*, that the character named the Author addresses his audience directly, posing the problems of staging an "improvised" play, lamenting the unruliness of his characters and the caprice of the stage technicians, and dramatizing the conflict between an author's illusory creation and the actors' living reality. When the curtain rises, all of the characters are on stage, waiting for something to happen. The Author steps forward to speak first. He explains that he has not been able to finish writing the evening's play (that is, it is a true improvisation), and that the troupe is counting on audience participation to make it a success.

Speaking metaphorically of the theater as a game in which a ball is passed back and forth between the actors and the spectators, the Author refers bitterly to audience air pockets filled with unskillful players who do not know how to send the ball back, and suggests that rehearsals include not only actors but audiences and critics as well. Finally, he pleads with the spectators not to take advantage of the intermission to leave the theater, because without them there is no hope of finishing the play.

III   *Invented Characters*

Another problem revealed to the audience of *La Grotte* is that of the difficulties encountered by a dramatist (as opposed to a novelist who can speak in his characters' stead) in expressing himself through his characters. The Director had wanted to eliminate the character of the Seminarist from *La Grotte* because he was unable to play a convincing love scene with Adèle, but the Author

was obliged to keep him because, just like Pirandello's Six Characters, the Seminarist has already taken thorny shape in the Author's
mind, and his existence cannot be wished away or denied.

The police chief is another troublesome character: he insists
upon addressing Adèle in a scene in which she is supposed to be
out of the country. The Author is chagrined, too, by Marie-
Jeanne, the cook, whom he had conceived as a female Falstaff but
who has nothing Shakespearian about her. He is aghast at the
idiotic lines uttered by some of the characters, realizing that
people might think that *he* wrote them. Moreover, some of the
characters have not even spoken yet because the Author has not
succeeded in embodying them in appropriate actors.

To intensify this dilemma, at a certain point in the play all of
the characters disappear and the Seminarist, on their behalf, approaches the Author to explain that the characters, rather than be
dishonest with themselves in playing their roles as the Author
conceives them, prefer to withdraw to nothingness. However,
since they have already begun to live, they will have to finish out
their roles, and request no further interference from the Author.
The Author apologizes for having invented the characters and
having interfered with their lives, to which the Seminarist retorts
that without him the characters might perhaps never have lived at
all. The characters' point is made, however, for after the Author
has taken his "coffee break" (the intermission of the play), he
returns to the theater to find the characters talking without him
and the audience, to his dismay, listening without coughing!

When a dramatist "invents" his characters, he is faced with the
problem of coordinating principal and secondary personages in a
given play. An imbalance among them will yield a poor drama, in
which the protagonist may appear disproportionately "heroic"
compared with the insignificant and grotesque secondary characters. If it is true that Anouilh erred in this respect in his early plays
(with the exception of *Le Bal des voleurs*)[5] it is also true that,
after 1936, the year in which the playwright discovered the art of
improvising plots and "playing" with his characters, their passions
and their intrigues,[6] the principal and secondary personages in his
plays form a balanced ensemble.

In *Antigone*, for example, even though the heroine stands apart
from Creon, Ismene, and Haemon, all play an essential role, and
the audience is constantly tempted to look with favor on each of

them. In *Pauvre Bitos,* Bitos, the figure of hatred, is meaningless without Camille, the figure of love, and without the entire cast that participates in the creation of the illusion of Robespierre's world. Similarly, in *Becket,* King Henry and Becket's mistress, Gwendolyn, are as significant and central as the hero.

Aware, then, of the disadvantages of having "stars" in a play or in a troupe of actors, and of the advantages of theatrical ensembles that utilize skill to the maximum and reduce dispersal of effort to the minimum, Anouilh has striven to attract a limited group of interpreters and actors; they have worked consistently and effectively with him throughout the years, principally in two or three theaters, in a close relationship that approaches the ideal of the *commedia dell'arte.* In a further effort to create "total" stage productions, Anouilh decided to become himself a *metteur-en-scène.* He had observed painfully that dramatic technique in France since the Second World War was sorely in need of being reanimated.

IV   *"Ballet" Plays*

Anouilh's plays have sometimes been called "ballets." The term is warranted, for frequently his plays are conceived as light, fantastic dances, with music an intrinsic part of them. The music for *L'Invitation au Château,* composed by Francis Poulenc, serves, as did the music for the *commedia dell'arte* scenarios, both to link the developments of the play and to add comic effects. At the beginning of Act II, for example, the tuning of the violins definitely marks the advancement of time since Isabelle's arrival in the morning, and the continual waltz music throughout the act indicates that the party is in progress. When, however, the orchestra takes up a duet entitled "The Waltz of the Little Moles," or a Mexican dance, or the "heroic, combative theme" in honor of Messerschmann and his daughter, comic effects are achieved. Poulenc also wrote the background waltz for *Léocadia:* the third tableau is a rehearsal of Léocadia's entrance into the café, to the strains of the "Blue Danube Waltz," by the maître d'hôtel and Amanda, and the fourth tableau is executed ironically as "a little furtive, jog-trotting ballet" on the waltz theme.

In the fifth tableau of *Le Voyageur sans bagage,* music by Darius Milhaud serves as an interlude between Gaston's unhappy interview with Valentine and the hopeful arrival of the little Eton schoolboy, Gaston's uncle. Later, the music assumes a mocking tone as the little boy reveals to Gaston that the members of his family and their intimate friends are all dead. Gaston's solemn entrance into the presence of the Duchess to prove his relationship to Master Pickwick is accompanied by a significant tremolo from the orchestra, and the play ends with a few bars of triumphant music.

Aside from the musical accompaniments, the entrances and exits of the characters, their steps, their movements, or their dances also reveal that Anouilh indeed conceived of some of his plays as ballets and carefully prepared the choreography. In *Le Bal des voleurs,* detailed annotations are given for the rhythms and dance steps of the thieves, the police, etc. In the third tableau, Lady Hurf calls out "To the ball! To the ball!" as the characters dance a quadrille off the stage. In the fourth tableau, Anouilh prescribes a comical ballet for the scene in which the DuPont-Duforts are arrested, and the play closes with a finale in double-quick time, as the entire cast dances on stage, exchanging their false beards.

Thus, several of Anouilh's plays may be characterized as "charades with music," [7] which, in essence, is a description of the unspoken parts of the *commedia dell'arte.* In fact, most of his plays give the clear impression that the dramatist is manipulating his stock characters in various ways, guiding them through a comic or tragic obstacle course of his own creation. The "pink" marionettes succeed, to the cheers of the audience; the "black" ones go down in defeat, and the audience weeps, but the following play brings them to life again in the eternal charades of stereotyped marionettes.

V *Divertissement*

Anouilh's dramatic *ars poetica* is contained in *Le Songe du critique,* in which he contrasts the fears of his antagonist (the Critic) that theatrical trends are toward "popular," facile, and diverting forms, with Anouilh's own hopes that the theater may become just that—a pure divertissement. The "educated" Critic, a pedant, worries unduly about the dramatic rules of the French Academy, objects to the playwright-turned-director, and reproaches the protagonist for his haphazard and improvised approach to the staging of a play without a solid theoretical construct. The Critic maintains that audiences have neither the time nor the right to go to the theaters today to be amused, for the world is plagued with many serious problems and the planet is threatened with nuclear destruction.

If a producer has no theory and no message to satisfy contemporary man's conscience, his voice, like the voice of racists and fascists, should be stilled, according to the Critic. Anouilh, however, is proud to define his purpose in presenting plays as solely to divert, for he realizes that the problems before the world are so serious, the questions of right and wrong so ambiguous, and the human predicament so untranslatable, that unless we are permitted to laugh at them they are not only unsolvable but intolerable.

To the Critic's objection that Anouilh takes liberties in clothing Molière's characters in twentieth-century costume, the defense lies in the reasonableness of clothing all bourgeois, of any era, in similar attire. To the criticism that a young actor playing the role of Tartuffe does not fit the concept of the older classical actors who usually assumed the role, Anouilh replies that the hypocrite Tartuffe has no age, that only circumstances change.

The presentation of *Tartuffe* that followed *Le Songe du critique* at the Comédie des Champs-Elysées in 1960 was, then, an example of Anouilh's concept of a dramatic technique that permits the dramatist to "play" with his marionettes, that survives through the ages, and that will serve the "theater of tomorrow" just as it has served the theater of the past. The play that diverts survives; characters that survive continue to divert.

In *Ornifle,* contemporary characters are dressed in seventeenth-century costume, preparatory to attending a "Molière party" at the home of a friend. Ornifle has assumed the role of the Misanthrope, and his two private physicians, in their black robes, ruffs, and pointed hats, are reminiscent of the doctors in Molière's *Le Malade imaginaire*. Their medical examination of Ornifle is ridiculous. Twentieth-century physicians are no more capable of diagnosing their patients' diseases than were their earlier counterparts. They are atavisms of the eternal Doctor Baloardos of the *commedia dell'arte*.

VI *The Play Within a Play*

The insertion of the "Molière party" into *Ornifle*, however, if not a cure for the ailing patient, is at least a form of escape from his boredom, and this is frequently the function of the play within a play in Anouilh's theater. Nine of the dramatist's works contain a play within them. In some cases the interpolated play is an actual or imaginary piece of literature (*La Répétition* and *Ornifle* contain, respectively, scenes from Marivaux and Molière, and *Colombe* includes an imaginary play, *La Maréchale d'Amour*, written in honor of Madame Alexandra). In other cases, the play within the play is an improvisation by the characters of the outer play.

In the second group, all of the *pièces roses* may be cited. Lady Hurf, in *Le Bal des voleurs*, is the stage director for the comedy in which she will star together with the imaginary Duc de Miraflor and his Spanish nobles. She introduces each actor individually and by name, and then all play their roles in *commedia dell'arte* style in the marionette world of her illusion. In *Le Rendez-vous de Senlis* the professional actors are thoroughly instructed in their roles by Georges, who is creating an ideal family to present to his beloved Isabelle.

Philémon, the actor hired by Georges, at first completely misunderstands his employer's concept of an ideal father, and disguises himself as a wrinkled, bearded octogenarian; this permits Georges to expostulate upon the necessity of molding an image around the concept in Isabelle's mind: a completely different father who is already half alive because someone believes that he exists. *Léocadia* is a series of acts within acts, as Amanda sometimes plays the role of the Italian diva and sometimes reverts to her true self. Anouilh places the young milliner on the stage of Pont-au-Bronc, where even the plants, the birds and the taxi-dwelling rabbits seem to be playing their assigned roles in the fantasy.

The play within a play in *L'Invitation au Château* is the improvised presentation planned by Horace. He tells the humble Isabelle, whom he has molded into the radiant young society woman expected by her audience, that he is depending on her ability to improvise during the performance. Isabelle and Horace succeed in delicately balancing the five acts of the play in a theatrical artifice that moves with the speed and the variegations of a ticktacktoe game on the squares of Harlequin's costume. The unwritten play within a play in *Pauvre Bitos* is the wig party, the perform-ance in which the diners relive the Reign of Terror. When Bitos faints, his real self is subordinated to the character under the wig: Robespierre. Here, as in *La Grotte*, the illusion of the "invented" characters' play triumphs over the Author's play.

Thus, the unreal, grotesque, and pathetically diverting charac-ters and situations in Anouilh's plays link his fantasy with that of the *commedia dell'arte*. His modern French protagonists are simi-lar to ancient zanies and Harlequins; they defend themselves against threatening "reason"; they answer with a grimace and a sneer the warnings and menaces of Captain Spaventos under all of his guises; they avenge the poor with their instinctively plebe-ian art. By his choice of melancholy stock characters combined with a technique of spontaneously complicating and unraveling extravagant plots, Anouilh has recaptured the spirit of the *com-media dell'arte*'s kaleidoscopic inventiveness, its improvisation, and its mixture of Maccus and Bucco.

CHAPTER 9

Theatrical Influences on Jean Anouilh

THE *commedia dell'arte,* Molière with his ability to evoke laughter at man's misery, and Marivaux and Musset with their theatrical escapes from reality—all are forebears of Jean Anouilh. From his own generation, Anouilh borrowed and intertwined opposing forces of convention and revolt. The three theatrical styles—realistic, popular, and "art"—to which he was exposed during his formative years as a playwright, all marked his plays in some way. The influence of the realistic Théâtre Libre and of the popular Théâtre du Boulevard has been noted in Chapter 1.

Among his immediate dramatic predecessors, it was the highly poetic playwright of the "Théâtre de l'Art," Jean Giraudoux, who was to wield one of the strongest influences on Anouilh. Giraudoux's *Siegfried,* inspired by the episode of an amnesia victim whose return to his native town after World War I caused great emotional upset in France, has obvious affinities with Anouilh's dramas of personal conflict and decision: *Y avait un prisonnier* and *Le Voyageur sans bagage.* Another theme basic to many of Anouilh's plays may be found in Giraudoux's *Ondine* (1939). The play is a commentary on man's attempt to reach perfection in the realm of the ideal; since his goal is unattainable, a tragic ending is inevitable.

I *Anouilh's Contemporaries*

Two Giraudoux plays, *Intermezzo* (1933) and *La Folle de Chaillot* (1945), examine the conflict between illusion and reality, blending fantasy and comedy with serious undertones. Also, Giraudoux's young heroines, pure, virtuous, innocent, radiant, and intransigent, who spin magic webs around themselves in order to shut out the prosaism of routine existence, find sister souls in Anouilh's lonely heroines; they speak the same poetic language and strive toward the same goal: the enthronement of an illusion.

131

Revolt against the status quo and the desire for escape are the dominant themes that find expression among twentieth-century French playwrights. The masks of bourgeois hypocrisy had been stripped off by the realities of two wars. What the mask had covered was unwholesome, disillusioning, nauseating. Solitude and anguish became the visible traits in the face of modern man. Desperately, he sought some justification for his existence and some ideal for which to strive. General and humane "causes" succeeded only in further intensifying his disillusionment, for every cause has its contingencies, and demands some compromise. Love itself quickly degenerates into falsity. Turning to his inner self, modern man is forced to contemplate an unrecognizable *persona* eroded by society and in a process of decay. Humanity, God, science—all are to blame for having relegated individual man to isolation and abandonment. Man's only responsibility, then, is to himself—a self-created image of himself, recognizable and tolerable to himself. He may choose subsequently to refuse the image and deliberately invite death, but the choice is his. He may concoct an absurd ideal, or reverse time, or live an illogical life-style in order to justify his existence and to defy the relativity of truth. Or he may find a solution in some form of escape that deflects him from total despair.

For Anouilh and many other modern dramatists, death is no guarantee that life's horrors are ended. In *L'Inconnue d'Arras* by Armand Salacrou, for example, the Man, who has just shot himself, is about to see his entire past life in review before dying. He objects to this imposition that prevents him from shedding the past even at the moment of death: "But I don't want to know anything anymore. I wanted to die, and now everything is starting all over again." [1] His protest is echoed by Anouilh's Eurydice, who is forced by Orpheus to relive her ugly past after she has been brought back to life by the mysterious Monsieur Henri. Salacrou had also treated the theme of the couple and pure love with an anguish similar to Anouilh's. In *Sens interdit,* Salacrou demonstrates that there is no "one and only" love, and that love, like every other ideal, degenerates with living. The adult world exerts a corrupting influence on the happy, because they are obsessed with the idea of degradation in time—themes that recur throughout all of Anouilh's *pièces grinçantes,* and particularly in *Ardèle.*

The theme of the irreversibility of time had been both comically and tragically expressed in Samuel Beckett's *En attendant Godot,* a play set midway between fiction and reality. At some time in the "past," an appointment had been made by two vagabonds with an invisible and elusive character, Godot. During the entire play, the two friends patiently await the arrival of Godot, who repeatedly sends a messenger to postpone the appointment. (Godot is comparable to Anouilh's sleeping God.) The daily incidents that occur have no relationship to the two tramps' conception of time: for them, the past is their present. Like Anouilh's pseudo-heroes, they believe in the reversibility of time, and continue to await the appointment in the past.

Marcel Achard had illustrated the theme of the relativity of truth in *Voulez-vous jouer avec moi?,* a play which, revolving around the theme of self-identity, is analogous to *Le Bal des voleurs.* Each of three circus clowns, believing himself loved by Isabelle, acts according to his own particular capacities to further endear himself to her. The behavior of each is ridiculous in relation to that of the other two, especially since Isabelle remains forever "undecided." Monsieur Loyal, a mute, immobile character who stands backstage—and is all the more insensitive to the frivolity of the clowns because he is made of wood—is the symbol of absolute truth.

The theme of escape had been cleverly summarized in the preface of Jean-Victor Pellerin's *Intimité:* "The Savage: How do you manage? The Civilized Man: I escape." [2] This one-act play, which has similarities to many of Anouilh's plays, is Pellerin's attempt to materialize the subconscious of the civilized man who lives by continual escape, finding it impossible to live honestly and harmoniously with even his most intimate companions. Without any physical movement on their part, both "Monsieur" and "Madame" mentally hasten to their respective *"rendez-vous de Senlis"*—an escape that renders their lives bearable. Another Pellerin play, *Têtes de rechange,* offered Anouilh an excellent illustration of the theme of multiple personality as a form of escape. The innumerable aspects of two rather ordinary beings, Ixe and Opeku, are presented, but the particular personality they will reveal in each scene is regulated by a lever that plays a role similar to that of a Lady Hurf; the lever manipulates the puppets Ixe and

Opeku and permits them momentarily to escape (depending upon its position on "work," "leisure," or "dead center") to their other selves.

Bava l'Africain by Bernard Zimmer had provided for Anouilh a magnificent example of the triumph of illusion over reality. The hero, Bava, has created an illusion that dominates his own life and mystifies those who know him and inevitably consider him mad: Bava claims to have been the personal companion of Savorgnan de Brazza in numerous African campaigns. At the end of the play, Bava, on his deathbed, is granted his last request. Everyone will accept his epitaph: "He dreamed dreams all his life, and he died embroiled in his dream. . . . Let us respect his dream up to the very end." [3] This epitaph might easily be transcribed onto the tombstones of Anouilh's heroes and heroines.

II   *Influence of Pirandello*

Despite the influences of many French playwrights, the one dramatist who seems to have had the greatest theatrical influence on Jean Anouilh was an Italian, namely Luigi Pirandello (1867–1936). [4] That Anouilh recognized Pirandello's importance and originality as a creator of modern drama is supported by his statements in 1952 and 1953 to the effect that *Six Characters in Search of an Author* was the play that swept the French stage clean of the dead débris of conventional drama. [5]

Anouilh's play *La Grotte*, with its "invented" characters, its mysterious murder, its artificially created suspense and its improvisations, is so evocative of Pirandello's *Six Characters, Ciascuno a suo modo* (*Each In His Own Way*), *Così è se vi pare* (*Right You Are If You Think You Are*), and *Questa sera si recita a soggetto* (*Tonight We Improvise*), that the Author anticipates, in the opening scene, that the audience will be whispering that they have already seen all of this in Pirandello. [6]

Beware of your reality; it is destined to become the illusion of tomorrow, warns the Father in *Six Characters in Search of an Author*. The action of the play unfolds on the levels of both reality and illusion: the Director, the actors and the actresses, rehearsing one of Pirandello's plays, represent the plane of reality; the weird appearance of the Six Characters bathed in a greenish light represents the plane of illusion. Interrupting the rehearsal, the Six Characters partly relate, partly enact, their tragic drama.

The incomplete drama within the Characters, which is gasping for expression, totally absorbs and overwhelms the "real" actors, who attempt to duplicate in their acting the drama of the Six; the final scene, in which the little girl is drowned and the young man shoots himself, causes the plane of reality to disappear completely: illusion emerges victorious, the hero of the play. Anouilh's *La Grotte*, as we have already seen, is also constructed on two planes—the universe of the upstairs and the downstairs kitchen— and the lighting forms an intrinsic part of the struggle between illusion and reality.

Many of Pirandello's dramas are based on the theme of illusion versus reality: *La Vita che ti diedi* (*The Life I Gave You*) revolves entirely around the necessity of constructing an illusion for oneself in order to bear routine existence. In this, it is comparable to the *pièces costumées*, and to *Léocadia*, in which the Prince and his entourage similarly live in an illusory world after the death of Léocadia Gardi, each for a different reason, but all so gripped by the power of their illusion that the reality of the outside world no longer exists for them. In *La Valse des Toréadors*, the General and Mademoiselle de Sainte-Euverte likewise fondle an illusion for almost twenty years, deriving from it the strength to endure their unattractive lives.

Illusions in other Pirandello and Anouilh plays also bear comparison. *Enrico IV* (*Henry IV*) opens with the appearance of Henry IV's councilors and valets, in authentic costume, discussing events of the eleventh century. We soon learn that the entire presentation is a fiction; that the man who pretends he is Henry IV has been insane for many years, owing to the perfidious accident caused by a certain Baron Belcredi; that Henry's wealthy relative, out of pity, allows him to live in his majestic illusion; that no one except Henry IV believes he is the German emperor. The cerebral injury caused by Henry's accident gives rise to the hero's illusion of an emperor's power and the cessation of time, but simultaneously provides a viable escape from society. The pretending Henry IV, realizing that time has rendered him incapable of manifesting his true self, his love, and his ideals, stabs Belcredi to death and then quickly escapes back into his madness. Similarly, Bitos' fainting spell animates the illusion of a dictator's power and the reversal of time; Prince Albert Trobiscoï, in *Léocadia*, and Georges, in *Le Rendez-vous de Senlis*, recall Henry IV in their feigned madness, which is their *cordon sanitaire* against society's horrors.

The theme of escape, linked with the irreversibility of time, is hauntingly expressed in *La Signora Morli una e due* (*Mrs. Morli, One and Two*), which has basic similarities with *Y avait un prisonnier*. Ferrante Morli, returning to his wife after a fifteen-year absence in America, finds circumstances and his wife so different from what he had left behind that he cannot accept "the present" as reality. Such is Ludovic's predicament, too, when he is released from jail and finds that his "present" is far removed from that of his family. In both plays, the vicissitudes of long years of life are concentrated into the space of a few hours to show the ravaging effects of time.

Other Pirandello and Anouilh plays have obvious thematic affinities. Both *Come tu mi vuoi* (*As You Desire Me*) and *Le Voyageur sans bagage* present an amnesia victim whose past is a mystery and who is being claimed by a supposed relative for reintegration into an unfamiliar family. Both plays present the struggle of the heroes against petty manifestations of the so-called "truth" of the past—a truth that demands the destruction of the happiness and tranquility for which they are striving. Harassed by those who relentlessly try to force them into an undesirable past, Pirandello's Strange Lady and Anouilh's Gaston wearily rebel. The Strange Lady's struggle ends in black defeat. For Gaston, who is a bit shrewder in evading his foes, the struggle ends in a form of escape, but the play remains pessimistic by the very nature of its theme.

The world of naïveté inhabited by Martino Lori in *Tutto per bene* (*All's For the Best*), with his self-imposed illusion that all is well even after shocking discoveries destroy his most cherished hopes, is the world to which the General in *L'Hurluberlu* escapes after the collapse of his secret society for the abolition of the world's corruption and after the destruction of his illusion of retaining his wife's love. Ersilia Drei's illusory concept of a dress that will cover the ugly truth of her past and spare her from dying "naked," in *Vestire gli Ignudi* (*To Clothe the Naked*), is comparable to the symbolic white gown Jeannette desires to wear in her lover's presence (*Roméo et Jeannette*), to Thérèse's elaborate wedding gown symbolic of a new life divorced from the past (*La Sauvage*), and to Eurydice's baptismal cloak of death.

Vivid illustrations of the important Pirandellian theme of multiple personality and of Baldovino's theory that we "make ourselves over" in accordance with the particular circumstances we happen to be in [*Il Piacere dell'onestà* (*The Pleasure of Being Honest*)] [7] are the characters of *Le Bal des voleurs* and *La Foire d'empoigne*. The multiple personality theme is closely linked with that of the relativity of truth, best demonstrated in Pirandello's well-known play *Così è se vi pare*, produced in English under the title of *Right You Are If You Think You Are*, in which "the truth" turns out to be whatever you choose.

In addition to plots and characters, Pirandello's dramatic technique was also a probable influence on Jean Anouilh. For example, in the "theater within the theater" trilogy (*Six Characters in Search of an Author, Tonight We Improvise* and *Each In His Own Way*), Anouilh must have seen the technique of the dramatist-puppeteer who plays with his "real" and "unreal" characters, their "true" and "illusory" situations, to the point where the two become inextricable. Pirandello used techniques of the *commedia dell'arte* freely, and in two of his plays (*Tonight We Improvise* and *Each In His Own Way*) makes specific references to the advantages of *commedia* improvisations, actors skillful in "ad-libbing," the use of masks, etc.[8]

The use of the mask or counterfeit personality serves similar purposes for Pirandello and Anouilh. In some cases the mask actually helps to uncover one's true feelings and allows the "true" self to emerge. In other cases, the mask is used to deal with the broader question of the human personality and its multiple facets. Preoccupied with the ambivalent nature of man's ever-changing personality, Pirandello and Anouilh create characters who are under perpetual tension and are obsessed with trying to understand themselves.

Both Pirandello and Anouilh, then, are in the *commedia dell'arte* tradition; both treat similar themes; and both dramatists were "launched" onto the Parisian stage by the *metteur-en-scène* Georges Pitoëff. From the many close parallels and the striking similarities of detail and overall atmosphere that may be drawn between the works of the two playwrights, we may conclude that, of all the dramatic and literary influences undergone by Jean Anouilh, that of Luigi Pirandello was the strongest.

CHAPTER 10

Conclusion

TO draw any definitive conclusion from the voluminous and diversified work of Jean Anouilh would be to limit the scope of his thought; yet forcefully present as the underlying conflict in most of his dramas is the hero's insistence on remaining pure and intransigent in the midst of corruption and compromise.

Although sensitive to the problems of the world, Anouilh offers neither a practical solution nor a message that might at least help us manage our hateful world. He is undoubtedly deeply concerned with the unhappy human condition, yet declines the palliatives that the world serves on a platter for mass consumption. Anouilh prefers ideals of his own making, according to his own recipes; if they are indigestible for many, they are nevertheless spiritually nutritious for a few—those few whose childlike image of a beautiful life prevents them from adapting to the relentless infernal machine.

Anouilh sees the masses as relegated to a limbo of mediocrity; they have never received the benefits of baptism by fire, blood, or even water to wash away their *sale bonheur*. Those, on the other hand, who have been baptized are clothed in a supernatural purity that thrusts them with centrifugal force toward an absolute to which they have aspired since childhood. Their escape from limbo and their struggle to realize their ideal give an incontestable dramatic force to Anouilh's plays; this force diminishes, however, when the heroic characters compromise, even though they realize with bad conscience, nostalgia, and even sadness that they have been unable to face the test of fire and blood.

In historic perspective, Anouilh will take his place among the mid-century pessimistic writers who have given vent to their disorientation, feelings of guilt, anguish, dissatisfaction, and disillusionment. The spirit of revolt has been discernible since Anouilh began writing. Two world wars together with unjustifiable local wars have deepened man's solitude, embittered him against the external world, and set him in search of a demanding morality based upon anything but bourgeois formulae. Anouilh's voice memorably, although perhaps at times too melodramatically, caricatures, disavows and demolishes society, and damns humanity. His "black" plays are Armageddons in which pure, pallid heroes oppose society's malevolence in a suicidal but crucial conflict. The lighter plays that offer escape into illusions are poetic refusals to fight.

Anouilh's work reflects the same mood that inspired the existentialism of Jean-Paul Sartre and Gabriel Marcel and the concept of the absurd [1]; his characters make the same gratuitous decisions as the existentialist heroes. The originality of Anouilh's heroes, however, lies in the timelessness of their decision-making process. No gesture, nor any action, has immediacy; past, present, and future intervene indiscriminately, leaving unaltered the inexorability of the hero's role.

The eternal quality of the characters and their endless search for purity transcends all events and circumstances; their inner development or spiritual evolution leads to a preconceived denouement and conclusion of a play, regardless of what the outside world proposes. Nothing the world can do suffices to attract the Anouilh hero centripetally into its orbit; nowhere in the world can he find the inner harmony that reflects unity in time and space (godliness). Still he embraces those very human elements which he finds hateful, for he is part of them and they may help him to gain a better knowledge of his true self; he may confess and purge himself through them. His final penance will result in the vindication of a universal heroic race that comprehends, but will not compromise.

Throughout the centuries spanned in Anouilh's dramas, although the gap between what is evil and what is good narrows, and the distinction between God's honor and the King's honor disappears, the ultimate choice between self-prostitution and acceptance of death in order to escape the common destiny is rigidly fixed. Betrayal of one's true self in legendary Greece, during the Inquisition, and in the twentieth century is identical. No character, no prop, no external circumstance can be anachronistic. Jean Anouilh's characters are easily identifiable with the present generation in their revolt; the situations which he creates give witness to an unending conflict between self and society. The canon of his plays mirrors both the mire that swallows the "pure" nonconformist and the pride that saves him.

As "*mininistatfia*" goes modern and as society becomes more mechanized and more scientific, the intransigent Anouilh hero may become even more meaningful. As the selector-processes and central data files diminish the importance of individual physical traits and lead toward the depersonalization of human beings, the constraints and obligations of position, maturity, and experience also diminish. Aware that his individuality is being replaced by a "punch card" that will be his sole means of identification, modern man is gaining a certain freedom which leads him to revert to the stereotype of the old *commedia dell'arte;* as such, he fears less the dangers of compliance and resignation that threaten his identity, and relates more easily to absolutes.

Anouilh will also be remembered as a dramatic ballet master who has marked the world of the stage with a particular brand of theatricality characterized by a return to the "playing" technique of the *commedia dell'arte.* Both his personal styling of "invented" characters and their vigorous dialogue as well merit emulation. He is a playwright who is also a craftsman of the theater. His unusual skill in presenting balanced menus of intellectual and philosophical food for thought with masterful doses of effective dramatic style and expression assures Anouilh's reputation as one of France's outstanding playwrights of this century.

Notes and References

Chapter One

1. Harold Clurman, *The Naked Image: Observations on the Modern Theatre* (New York: Macmillan, 1966), p. 31.

2. Jean Anouilh, *Nouvelles pièces noires* (Paris: La Table ronde, 1958), p. 363.

3. Jean-Louis Barrault, "Depuis Chaptal . . ." *Cahiers de la Compagnie Madeleine Renaud—Jean-Louis Barrault*, Vol. 26 (May, 1959), pp. 45, 47.

4. Paul-Louis Mignon, "Le Théâtre de A jusqu'à Z: Jean Anouilh," *L'Avant-Scène*, No. 210 (December 15, 1959), p. 6.

5. *Ibid.*

6. See the Chronology above for film rights sold to Hollywood. Some of Anouilh's well-known French film scripts are: *Caroline Chérie, Cavalcade d'Amour, Monsieur Vincent, Anna Karénine, Deux sous de violettes.*

7. Anouilh, *Pièces brillantes* (Paris: La Table ronde, 1951), p. 192.

8. *L'Hurluberlu*, p. 199.

9. Anouilh, *Pièces costumées* (Paris: La Table ronde, 1960), p. 162.

10. *Pièces brillantes*, p. 515.

11. *Ibid.*, p. 40.

12. *Ibid.*

13. Jean-Pierre Lassalle, *Jean Anouilh ou la vaine révolte* (Rodez: Editions Subervie, 1958), p. 41.

14. Clurman, *op. cit.*, p. 35.

15. In addition to his first and second wives, Anouilh's daughter Catherine is also an actress, and has played in several of her father's plays: *Cécile, Ornifle, La Petite Molière*, and a revival of *Ardèle*.

16. For example, Anouilh heaps contempt on the actor Philémon in *Le Rendez-vous de Senlis* who, thinking his salary is at stake, threatens to use his union connections to exact payment for his services.

17. *Le Figaro littéraire*, June 15, 1963, p. 6.

18. Joseph Barry, "A Walk and a Talk with Jean Anouilh," *New York Times*, September 13, 1964, § 2, p. 5.

19. Mignon, *op cit.*, p. 6.

Chapter Two

1. *Nouvelles pièces noires,* p. 279.
2. Anouilh, *Pièces grinçantes* (Paris: La Table ronde, 1957), p. 458.
3. *Nouvelles pièces noires,* p. 188.
4. *Pièces costumées,* p. 131.
5. *Ibid.,* p. 26.
6. *Ibid.,* p. 87.
7. *Ibid.,* p. 32.
8. *Ibid.,* p. 131.
9. *Nouvelles pièces noires,* p. 366.
10. *Ibid.,* p. 367.
11. *Ibid.,* p. 359.
12. *Ibid.,* p. 379.
13. Anouilh, *Oreste* (fragments) in Robert de Luppé, *Jean Anouilh, suivi des fragments de la pièce de Jean Anouilh: Oreste* (Paris: Editions universitaires, 1959), p. 115.
14. *Pièces brillantes,* p. 493.
15. *Nouvelles pièces noires,* p. 45.
16. This is a typically Pirandellian theme, as will be noted in Chapter 5.
17. These are the plays most clearly inspired by Jean Giraudoux.
18. Anouilh, *Pièces noires* (Paris: Calmann-Lévy, 1945), p. 209.
19. Anouilh, *Le Songe du critique, L'Avant-Scène,* No. 243 (May 15, 1961), p. 34.
20. *Pièces noires,* p. 360.
21. *Pièces costumées,* p. 184.
22. This is the message of the potato peeler in *La Grotte.*
23. *Pièces costumées,* p. 208.
24. *Ibid.,* p. 273.
25. *Ibid.,* p. 112.
26. *Ibid.,* p. 76.
27. *Ibid.,* p. 264.
28. *Nouvelles pièces noires,* p. 389.
29. *Pièces costumées,* p. 294.
30. Robert de Luppé, *Jean Anouilh* (Paris: Editions universitaires, 1959), p. 90.
31. Anouilh, *L'Hurluberlu* (Paris: La Table ronde, 1959), p. 91.
32. *Nouvelles pièces noires,* p. 177.
33. *Pièces grinçantes,* p. 437.
34. *Nouvelles pièces noires,* pp. 140, 143.
35. *Ibid.,* pp. 366–67.
36. *Pièces costumées,* p. 56.
37. *Ibid.,* p. 83.

38. Clurman, *op. cit.*, p. 142.
39. *Pièces grinçantes,* p. 277.

Chapter Three

1. *Nouvelles pièces noires,* p. 77.
2. *Ibid.*, p. 121.
3. *Pièces noires,* p. 210.
4. See above, Chapter 2, pp. 38ff.
5. *Pièces noires,* p. 169.
6. *Ibid.*, p. 176.
7. *Ibid.*, p. 192.
8. See above, Chapter 2, p. 29.
9. *Pièces noires,* p. 303.
10. Anouilh, *Y avait un prisonnier, La Petite Illustration,* No. 370 (May 18, 1935).
11. See above, Chapter 1, pp. 17ff.
12. Clurman, *op. cit.*, p. 32.
13. *Pièces noires,* p. 222.
14. *Ibid.*, p. 242.
15. *Ibid.*, p. 246.
16. *Ibid.*, p. 287.
17. *Nouvelles pièces noires,* p. 249.
18. *Ibid.*, p. 294.
19. *Ibid.*, p. 296.
20. *Ibid.*, p. 225.
21. Anouilh, *La Grotte* (Paris: La Table ronde, 1961), p. 141.
22. *Ibid.*, p. 50.
23. *Ibid.*, p. 51.
24. *Ibid.*, p. 55.
25. *Ibid.*, p. 97.
26. *Ibid.*, p. 146.

Chapter Four

1. *Life,* March 10, 1967, p. 82.
2. Anouilh, *Pièces roses* (Paris: Calmann-Lévy, 1942), p. 69.
3. *Ibid.*, p. 108.
4. See above, Chapter 3, pp. 55–56.
5. *Pièces roses,* p. 119.
6. *Ibid.*, p. 120.
7. *Ibid.*, p. 211.
8. *Ibid.*, p. 179.
9. *Ibid.*, p. 326.
10. *Ibid.*, p. 324.

Chapter Five

1. *Pièces brillantes,* p. 117.
2. *Ibid.*
3. As in *Pauvre Bitos* and *Ardèle.*
4. *Pièces brillantes,* p. 534.
5. *Ibid.,* p. 428.
6. See above, Chapter 2, pp. 36ff.
7. *Pièces brillantes,* p. 359.
8. *Ibid.,* p. 170.

Chapter Six

1. De Luppé, *op. cit.,* p. 90.
2. *Ardèle* and her lover.
3. See below, Chapter 5, p. 132.
4. *Pièces grinçantes,* p. 116.
5. *Ibid.,* p. 132.
6. *Ibid.,* p. 155.
7. *Ibid.,* p. 210.
8. *"Hurluberlu"* means a scatterbrained, rash, giddy individual; the subtitle of the play, the "amorous reactionary," is reminiscent of the subtitle of Molière's *Le Misanthrope,* the "amorous self-tormentor."
9. These are pointed references to de Gaulle, as mentioned above in Chapter 1.
10. *L'Hurluberlu,* p. 65.
11. Anouilh, *Ornifle* (Paris: La Table ronde, 1956), p. 95.
12. *Pièces grinçantes,* pp. 233–34.

Chapter Seven

1. In the program of the French production of *L'Alouette;* quoted in Christopher Fry's translation, *The Lark* (New York: Oxford University Press, 1956), p. ii.
2. *Nouvelles pièces noires,* p. 397.
3. *Pièces costumées,* p. 339.
4. *L'Hurluberlu,* p. 208.
5. *Nouvelles pièces noires,* p. 367.
6. *Ibid.,* p. 361.
7. *Ibid.,* p. 384.
8. *Ibid.,* p. 206.
9. *Ibid.,* p. 174.
10. *Ibid.,* p. 187.
11. *Oreste,* p. 106.
12. *Ibid.,* p. 116.

13. *Ibid.*, p. 115.
14. *Pièces costumées*, p. 29.
15. *Ibid.*, p. 19.
16. *Ibid.*, p. 27.
17. *Ibid.*, p. 109.
18. *Ibid.*, p. 273.
19. *Ibid.*, p. 295.
20. *Ibid.*, p. 187.
21. *Ibid.*, p. 175.
22. *Ibid.*, p. 329.
23. *Ibid.*, p. 371.
24. *Nouvelles pièces noires*, p. 372.
25. *Pièces grinçantes*, p. 437.

Chapter Eight

1. Mignon, *op. cit.*, p. 6.
2. *Pièces roses*, p. 132.
3. John Harvey, *Anouilh: A Study in Theatrics* (New Haven and London: Yale University Press, 1964), p. 5.
4. *La Grotte*, p. 103.
5. Cf. Serge Radine, *Anouilh, Lenormand, Salacrou: trois dramaturges à la recherche de leur vérité* (Geneva: Editions des trois collines, 1951), pp. 17–18.
6. Anouilh's revelation of his 1936 discovery appears in André Franck's article "Le Théâtre d'aujourd'hui: Jean Anouilh," *Les Nouvelles littéraires*, No. 962 (January 10, 1946), p. 2.
7. Christopher Fry has labeled *Ring 'Round the Moon* (London: Methuen, 1950), his adaptation of *L'Invitation au Château*, a "Charade with Music."

Chapter Nine

1. Armand Salacrou, *Théâtre* (Paris: Gallimard, 1942), p. 128.
2. Jean-Victor Pellerin, *Intimité* (Paris: Calmann-Lévy, 1929), p. i.
3. Bernard Zimmer, *Bava l'Africain*, 2d ed. (Paris: Gallimard, 1929), p. 125.
4. See Alba della Fazia, "Luigi Pirandello and Jean Anouilh" (unpublished Ph.D. dissertation, Columbia University, 1954).
5. See Jean Anouilh, "Que voilà une bonne pièce," *Le Figaro*, No. 2293 (January 23, 1952), p. 6; and Jean Anouilh, "*En attendant Godot* de Samuel Beckett," Théâtre de Babylone program, 1953.
6. For the following pages of this chapter, I have drawn from my article "Pirandello and His French Echo Anouilh," *Modern Drama* (February 1964), pp. 346–67 *passim*.

7. Luigi Pirandello, *Maschere Nude* (Milano: Mondadori, 1932–35), III, 148.

8. *Ibid.*, VI, 253; I, 183.

Chapter Ten

1. Cf. Edwin Owen Marsh, *Jean Anouilh: Poet of Pierrot and Pantaloon* (London: W. H. Allen, 1953), pp. 192 ff.; Serge Radine, *op. cit.*, pp. 23–27.

Selected Bibliography

PRIMARY SOURCES

Le Boulanger, la Boulangère et le Petit Mitron. Paris: La Table ronde, 1968.

Episode de la vie d'un auteur. *Cahiers de la Compagnie Madeleine Renaud—Jean-Louis Barrault*, Vol. 26 (May, 1959).

La Grotte. Paris: La Table ronde, 1961.

L'Hurluberlu. Paris: La Table ronde, 1959.

The Lark (*L'Alouette*). Translated by Christopher Fry. New York: Oxford University Press, 1956.

Nouvelles pièces noires: Jézabel, Antigone, Roméo et Jeannette, Médée. Paris: La Table ronde, 1958.

L'Orchestre. *L'Avant-Scène*, No. 276 (November 15, 1962), pp. 30–38.

Oreste (fragments). Robert de Luppé. *Jean Anouilh, suivi des fragments de la pièce de Jean Anouilh: Oreste*. Paris: Editions universitaires, 1959.

Ornifle, ou le Courant d'air. Paris: La Table ronde, 1956.

La Petite Molière. *L'Avant-Scène*, No. 210 (December 15, 1959), pp. 10–42.

Pièces brillantes: L'Invitation au Château, Colombe, La Répétition, ou l'Amour puni, Cécile, ou l'Ecole des pères. Paris: La Table ronde, 1951.

Pièces costumées: L'Alouette, Becket, ou l'Honneur de Dieu, La Foire d'empoigne. Paris: La Table ronde, 1960.

Pièces grinçantes: Ardèle, ou la Marguerite, La Valse des Toréadors, Ornifle, ou le Courant d'air, Pauvre Bitos, ou le Dîner de têtes. Paris: La Table ronde, 1957.

Pièces noires: L'Hermine, La Sauvage, Le Voyageur sans bagage, Eurydice. Paris: Calmann-Lévy, 1945.

Pièces roses: Le Bal des voleurs, Le Rendez-vous de Senlis, Léocadia. Paris: Calmann-Lévy, 1942.

Ring 'Round the Moon (*L'Invitation au Château*). Adapted by Christopher Fry, with a preface by Peter Brook. London: Methuen, 1950.

Le Songe du critique. L'Avant-Scène, No. 243 (May 15, 1961), pp. 31–35.

Y avait un prisonnier. La Petite Illustration, No. 370 (May 18, 1935).

SECONDARY SOURCES

BARRY, JOSEPH. "A Walk and a Talk with Jean Anouilh." *New York Times,* September 13, 1964, §2, pp. 1, 5. One of the few published interviews with Jean Anouilh, in which the playwright reveals several biographical facts and discusses his future intentions.

BORGAL, CLÉMENT. *Anouilh: La Peine de vivre.* Paris: Editions du Centurion, 1966. This latest critical work on Anouilh is a somewhat abstruse metaphysical analysis of the plays from the point of view of Christian dogma.

Cahiers de la Compagnie Madeleine Renaud—Jean-Louis Barrault, Vol. 26 (May, 1959). The entire issue of the quarterly is devoted to articles on Molière and Anouilh, and contains two Anouilh texts: the one-act play *Episode de la vie d'un auteur,* and the short story *Histoire de M. Mauvette et de la fin du monde.*

CLURMAN, HAROLD. *The Naked Image: Observations on the Modern Theatre.* New York: Macmillan, 1966. Perceptive analyses of today's playwrights. The section on Anouilh contains critiques of *The Fighting Cock (L'Hurluberlu), Becket* (Paris and New York productions), *Traveller Without Luggage,* and *Poor Bitos.*

DE LUPPÉ, ROBERT. *Jean Anouilh.* Paris: Editions universitaires, 1959. Analyzes many important themes in Anouilh's work, and includes discussions of the plays produced in the 1950's, which are lacking in the Gignoux and Marsh volumes. Good bibliography.

GIGNOUX, HUBERT. *Jean Anouilh.* Paris: Editions du Temps Présent, 1946. The author groups his analysis around five plays, *La Sauvage, Eurydice, Le Voyageur sans bagage, Antigone,* and *Le Rendez-vous de Senlis,* using the first as his focal point. The discussion of the plays is very clear, and the author maintains, as contrasted with Serge Radine *et al.,* that Anouilh stresses, and does not destroy, the highest moral and spiritual values.

GUICHARNAUD, JACQUES. *Modern French Theatre from Giraudoux to Beckett.* New Haven: Yale University Press, 1961. A good analysis of ten outstanding modern French dramatists whose heroes are alienated from society and refuse to conform to patterns established by human institutions, plus a much-needed chapter on modern farce. The chapter which interweaves Anouilh's and Salacrou's works indicates the similarities between the two playwrights.

HARVEY, JOHN. *Anouilh: A Study in Theatrics.* New Haven and London: Yale University Press, 1964. A highly theoretical and somewhat abstruse volume describing Anouilh's theory of drama; the theatricalist playwright's approach to form, style, and staging. Establishes theatricality as the unifying principle behind Anouilh's handling of plot, characters, and language, and as the key to the staging of his plays. Demonstrates that Anouilh's concern is not so much to represent the world *in* theater as to present the world *of* theater; his goal is not to *translate* reality but to *transpose* it.

HOBSON, HAROLD. *The French Theatre Today.* London: George C. Harrap, 1953. An Englishman's evaluation of living French masters of the theater, concentrating on Sartre, Montherlant, Salacrou, and Anouilh.

LASSALLE, JEAN-PIERRE. *Jean Anouilh ou la vaine révolte.* Rodez: Editions Subervie, 1958. This thin volume contains analyses of Anouilh's heroes as inhuman seekers of purification in the midst of a corrupt society. He describes the heroes as nonconstructive *révoltés* rather than constructive *révolutionnaires* and decries their individual acts.

MARSH, EDWIN OWEN. *Jean Anouilh: Poet of Pierrot and Pantaloon.* London: W. H. Allen, 1953. An introduction to Anouilh's theater for the general public. Each of Marsh's lengthy plot analyses is supported by an introduction and a conclusion, neither of which stresses sufficiently why Anouilh should be called a "poet of Pierrot and Pantaloon."

MIGNON, PAUL-LOUIS. "Le Théâtre de A jusqu'à Z: Jean Anouilh." *L'Avant-Scène,* No. 210 (December 15, 1959), p. 6. Another article that contains some of the few public statements made by Anouilh, from whom Mignon has elicited several remarks on dramatic concepts and style.

PRONKO, LEONARD CABELL. *The World of Jean Anouilh.* Berkeley and Los Angeles: University of California Press, 1961. Clearly written, well-organized and well-conceived. A good final chapter on the use of myth in Anouilh's theater.

RADINE, SERGE. *Anouilh, Lenormand, Salacrou; trois dramaturges à la recherche de leur vérité.* Geneva: Editions des trois collines, 1951. The author places Anouilh among the despairing "black" romantics of the nineteenth century. He draws an analogy between the Existentialists and Anouilh, and especially between Sartre's *Les Mains sales* and *Antigone.* The book stresses the weaknesses of Anouilh's dramaturgy and disputes the contention that Anouilh is a poet of Harlequin, in view of his extreme bitterness. Radine is a disappointed critic: he expected more of Anouilh, whom he accuses of being too close to the "boulevard" writers.

TOUCHARD, PIERRE-AIMÉ. Introduction to *Une pièce rose, deux pièces noires, par Jean Anouilh. Théâtre,* No. 6. Paris: Club des libraires de France, 1956. A good introduction to *Le Bal des voleurs, La Sauvage,* and *Eurydice.* Touchard explains the essence of Anouilh's "pink" and "black" theater in terms of the pre- and post-World War I and II periods.

Index

(References to Anouilh's works will be found under the author's name)

151